ROOM-BY-ROOM AFGHANS

ROOM-BY-ROOM AFGHANS

FORTY PROJECTS AND ACCESSORIES TO KNIT AND CROCHET

VALERIE KURITA

A GENIE BOOK

ST. MARTIN'S PRESS NEW YORK

Every effort has been made to ensure the accuracy
and clarity of the directions in this book. Although
we cannot be responsible for misinterpretations of
directions or variations caused by an individual's
working techniques, we would be happy to answer
any questions you may have about the instructions.
Address inquiries to the author, in care of Genie
Books, 218 Madison Avenue, New York, NY 10016.

Designed by Lily Lee and Miriam Haas
Photography by Philip Stark
Photography styling by Lily Lee

Library of Congress Cataloging in Publication Data
Kurita, Valerie.
    Room-by-room afghans
    1. Afghans (Coverlets)—Patterns. 2. House
furnishings.   I. Title.
TT825.K8674 1986   746.9'7   86-3998
ISBN 0-312-69281-1

To
Virginia Williams,
Grace Takakuwa,
Sandra Nishida,
and
Emi Kamiya,

who have been
a continuous source of encouragement
and inspiration for many years

ACKNOWLEDGMENTS

The author would like to thank Marie Jourdain and Jeannie Thibodeaux for their expert handwork. Extra special thanks go to Bertha Zeltser. Without her effort and support this book would not have been possible.
In addition, I'd like to give special thanks for the kind cooperation of Anne Bradley at Dupont Co. for help in obtaining Sayelle and Wintuk yarns for use in this book.

With great appreciation for allowing our crew, with a vanload of photographic equipment, to occupy his home for ten days, Genie Books thanks John B. P. Hood, whose lovely NYC brownstone was the location for the color photography in this book. We also thank his thirteen-year-old schnauzer, Chesterfield, for beginning his modeling career by enthusiastically sitting for our "Contemporary Living Room" photograph. Further gratitude goes to Wayne Marshall and his dog Sati for their respective performances in the "Contemporary Nursery" and the "Preppy Plaids for a Boy's Room" photographs. Finally, we wish to thank M & M Furniture Center, NYC, for the generous loan of their chair in the "Deco Master Bedroom" photograph, as well as Ben's Babyland, NYC, for the loan of the crib in the photograph of "Pocket Animal Nursery."

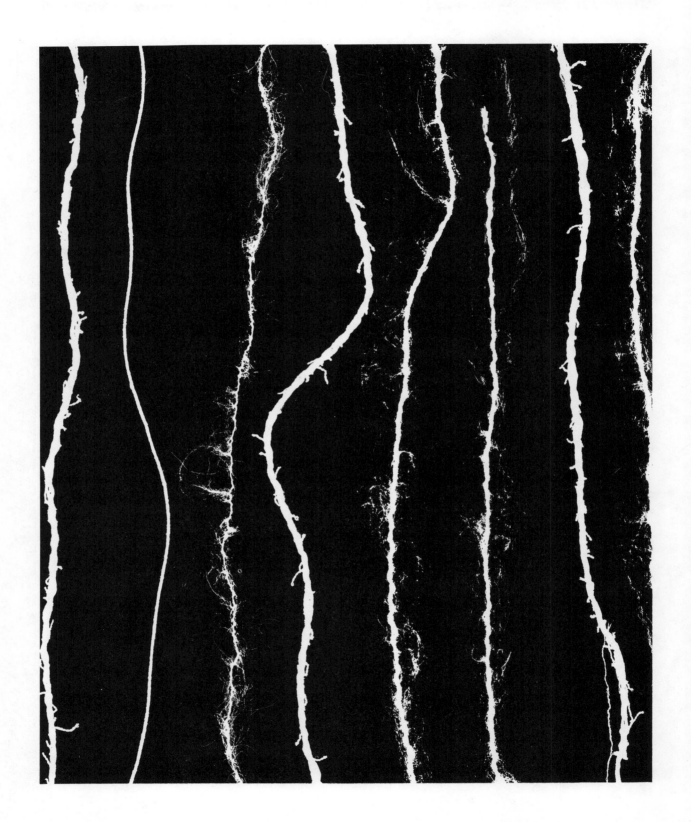

YARN-BUYING GUIDE

The author would like to thank the following yarn companies
for their courteous support and for the opportunity
to work with their beautiful yarns. If your local yarn shop
does not carry the yarn specified in the directions for our
projects, please write to the proper company below for
purchasing and ordering information:

Brunswick Yarns
Pickens, SC 29671

Coats & Clark Sales Corp.
72 Cummings Point Road
Stamford, CT 06902

Caron International, Inc.
Avenue E and South First Sts.
Rochelle, IL 61068

Lion Brand Yarn Company
1270 Broadway
New York, NY 10001

CONTENTS

INTRODUCTION

Afghans have always been one of the most, if not the most, popular projects for the knitter or crocheter. They are not only pleasant to make for oneself; they also, when given as a gift, show much love, considering the time required to hand-create an item that, by its very nature, sends a message of comfort and warmth to the receiver. Afghans, when made well, are durable and are often handed down from generation to generation. Many a homesick college student or young camper has been comforted by the presence of the familiar afghan that had lain at the foot of his bed during childhood.

As I meet handworkers these days, though, I find that while they would like to be able to spend the time to create an heirloom afghan, they are too pressed with the multiple responsibilities of family, career, and community. Consequently, requests for patterns that are quick and easy come from all over. To meet this need, I have designed this unique book of afghans and quick-to-make accessories.

For instance, you may wish to make the projects in the English Country grouping for the bedroom, but not have the time to complete the entire set of afghan, pillow, and footstool cover. Why not start with the pillow, which, by itself, makes a lovely gift item or decorative accent for your own home? Once you have learned the simple technique for duplicate stitch, you may be inspired to make the matching footstool and afghan when time permits. The same is true for any of the groupings.

I've tried to offer designs in this collection that will fit with a number of today's favorite decorating styles. There are projects suitable for French Provincial, Southwestern, Art Deco, Victorian, and contemporary rooms. Although I've designed the groupings with a special room in mind, feel free to put bedroom afghans in the living room and vice versa. In addition to these projects for the home, I've included a set of projects in both the knitted and crocheted sections for "On-the-Go." These are items designed so that you can have the comfort of home with you wherever you may travel. Suitable for warming up at outdoor sporting events, in air-conditioned movie theaters, in chilly cars, and on freezing airplanes, they make a much-used and appreciated gift.

Since these projects are bound to get frequent use, I've chosen yarns that are durable and washable. Another of my considerations was the cost and availability of the materials. Consequently, I've tried to use those yarns that are widely distributed in outlets and chain stores and that won't break the bank, taking into consideration the large amounts necessary to buy enough yarn to make an afghan or rug.

One more point—although I have often experienced a great deal of satisfaction from working complex knitted and crocheted patterns, I find that I very much enjoy doing designs that require little thinking, allowing me to watch television or talk with family or friends, or simply to let my mind wander. In accordance with this thought, I've tried to offer you many patterns that make the maximum design statement with the minimum of effort. For instance, with the English Country design, the stockinette stitch that forms the background of the afghan, pillow, and footstool projects can be done almost blindfolded. The duplicate stitch embroidery, of course, takes more attention, but it can be saved for a time when you have a little solitude.

I truly hope that this book has something for everyone and that you enjoy the beautiful decorating highlights any of the coordinated sets of afghans and accessories can bring to your loved ones, or to your own home.

Now, please take a moment to read the next few pages, which explain the format of the instructions and which will offer some tips on working and finishing your projects.

ABOUT OUR INSTRUCTIONS

In the fall of 1979, yarn industry and handknit and crochet professionals in publishing and fashion design gathered to standardize, as much as possible, the stitch abbreviations used by craft publications. The abbreviations they came up with have been used widely over the last years so that the consumer would not be confused by the variances in terminology that once occurred from publication to publication. Whenever you see the "Simplified Instructions" logo (see p. 21) in a magazine or book, you will know that these abbreviations have been followed.

Each of the twelve groupings of projects in this book has been photographed in color. Each of the forty projects included in the groupings has also been photographed individually in black-and-white to show design and stitch detail, which I hope will aid you in making the item.

Within each set of instructions you will find the following information:

Approximate finished size
Experience designation ("No experience needed," "Some experience needed," "Experience needed")
Project description
Required materials
Gauge
Working instructions
Charts or diagrams, where necessary

Each of the above items is important to consider in obtaining results you will be happy with.

The **approximate finished size** tells you, allowing for differences in working techniques, the measurements of your completed project. This information will be particularly helpful to you on those projects where you may need to make your own calculations for custom-designed sizes—for instance, on shelf edging or footstool covers—or just to change the size of an afghan.

The **experience designation** will help you decide whether or not this project is for you. If you are a beginner, I hope that you will begin with the simplest designs and graduate, step by step, to the more difficult. In any case, every stitch used in the patterns in this book is briefly explained in the "Stitch Glossary" in the back of the book. Although this is not a "how-to-knit and crochet" book, I think that any of the designs included are within the reach of most needleworkers and may help you advance in skill as you teach yourself new techniques. If you get stuck, remember that there are many books available that can help you with the basics but that there is no replacement for a "hands-on" teacher, be it a patient friend or relative, or a helpful yarn-shop owner.

In the brief **project description** accompanying each black-and-white photo, I try to describe the piece and offer some suggestions as to alternate uses, color substitutions, or other alterations that may be helpful to you.

The information provided under **required materials** is crucial to the success of your project. In all cases except for the Contemporary Living Room, the yarns used fall into the category of knitted worsted weight. The yarns I chose were graciously supplied by a number of national yarn companies; because the projects were designed specifically for these yarns, I recommend that they be used for best results. (See "Yarn-Buyer's Guide" for information on ordering by mail the yarns used in the patterns.) The brand name, color, and color number are clearly listed. Be sure to buy the total amount of yarn needed for your project so that the skeins will all be from the same dye lot. Many yarn-shop owners are willing to put away yarn in your dye lot for you so that you can buy it little by little, as needed. Needle or hook sizes and any material needed for stuffing or lining the finished piece are also listed in detail.

Although the **gauge** is not quite as important when making items for the home as it is when making fashion projects that must fit exactly, adherence to gauge will produce a fabric in the appropriate texture for the project. Always work a test swatch of at least four by four inches to determine your working gauge. If your test piece is smaller than the indicated size, use a larger hook or needle. If it is larger, use a smaller hook or needle. If you substitute a yarn other than the one called for in the instructions, be doubly sure that your gauge is correct to prevent such disasters as an afghan large enough to cover the garage or a crib blanket the size of a postage stamp.

I've tried to make the **working instructions** as clear as possible so that frustration is kept to a minimum. Should you have any questions, though, be sure to refer to the abbreviations list and the "Stitch Glossary." If you still need more help, please don't hesitate to write to me in care of Genie Books, 218 Madison Avenue, New York, NY 10016, and I'll answer you as soon as possible.

Charts and diagrams are largely self-explanatory, but keep in mind that you will be reading the rows on the charts from the bottom to the top in most cases. Right-side rows are usually the odd-numbered rows, and wrong-side rows, where shown, are even-numbered. Read the charts, stitch by stitch, from right to left for right-side rows and from left to right for wrong-side rows. Whenever the reading of the chart is different from the general instructions outlined here, there is a note to that effect.

Most of all relax and enjoy your knitting or crocheting. You'd be surprised at how much your gauge can tighten when you are tired or tense. (If you have a deadline for gift-giving, rest assured that you won't be the first needleworker to give an unfinished, gift-wrapped project, needles or hook and all, along with a note expressing your good intentions of finishing it at the earliest opportunity.)

FINISHING TECHNIQUES

In order to give your projects for the home the touch that says "handmade" and not "homemade," you'll need to know some fine points about finishing. These techniques will ensure that the appearance of your completed piece will attest to the effort and care you expended in its making.

Working Single-Crocheted Edgings

Occasionally, before components of a project are joined or after a whole afghan has been made, the edges will need to be finished with a row of single-crochet in order for the piece to lie flat and the edges to be absolutely even and regular. Usually it is up to the crocheter to determine the exact number of stitches necessary.

If you are working along the side of a knitted piece, work into a knot rather than a thread wherever possible so that holes won't be created along the finished edge. If you are working across the top or bottom edge of knitting, it is best to skip every third or fourth stitch instead of working into every one in order to prevent the edge from rippling. There will be a bit of tension in the edge, but when blocked, the piece will flatten perfectly. Be sure that the same number of stitches are worked along any two edges that are of equal length, and work three stitches in any corner.

Working Color-over-Color

On some projects, you may be asked to work a single-crocheted edging color-over-color or a fringe trim color-over-color. This means that you should match the color of the crochet or fringe to the color of the edge along which you are working. (See the crochet section in the "Stitch Glossary" to learn how to change colors in the middle of the row.)

Seaming

In most cases, the best way to ensure nearly invisible seams is to use a running back stitch or an overcast stitch (see "Stitch Glossary") on the wrong side of the work, matching stitch to stitch so that the patterns align and the work lies flat. When exceptions to this rule occur, the individual project instructions will guide you.

Blocking

There are some yarns, such as mohair, that by nature need

no blocking; many of the newer yarns also need none. Whenever blocking is essential to the design, however, it will be called for in the directions. For instance, squares knitted on a diagonal usually come out diamond-shaped; they must be blocked into shape before they can be edged and/or joined. In this case, shape the piece as desired, pin it to a padded board, and cover it with a damp towel. Then steam it by holding an iron in contact with the towel, never putting full pressure on the piece but allowing the steam to do the work. Let the pieces dry completely before removing them. When blocking is not stipulated, it is up to you whether to block or not, depending on the appearance of the seams and the overall look of the finished project.

Fringing

To knot fringe, insert a crochet hook from back to front through the stitch to be fringed, catch the middle of the group of fringe strands with the hook, and pull it partly through the stitch, making a loop. Catch all ends of the strands with the hook and pull them through the loop. Pull the ends to tighten the knot.

MAKING PILLOWS, RUGS, AND WALL HANGINGS

Many of the items in the coordinated sets of knitted and crocheted projects in this book are pillows, rugs, or wall hangings that will need some type of backing to make them durable. Knitted pieces that are to be used as rugs and wall hangings, in particular, do not have sufficient body by themselves. With each set of instructions, the amount of fabric, stuffing material, and other supplies needed to complete the projects are listed. Here, however, you will find the general sewing instructions needed to finish each type of item.

Making Pillows

Most of the pillows in this book are square (when there is an exception, specific instructions have been given). To make a square pillow, you will need to make a pillow form from the desired fabric. Complete the knitted or crocheted square (pillow front) as outlined in the project instructions. Measure the pillow front and cut from fabric two pieces that measure 1/2 inch more all around than the knitted or crocheted piece. With right sides of the two pieces of fabric facing, stitch a seam 1/2 inch in from the edges on three sides of the square. Stitching 1/2 inch in from the edge, sew the fourth side closed for about 2 inches at each corner. Turn the fabric pieces right side out and stuff the pillow form with polyester stuffing. Handsew the fourth side closed with slip stitches, turning under the raw edges as you work.

Now, place the knitted or crocheted pillow front, right side up, on the finished pillow form, with the edge of the pillow front slightly overlapping the edges of the form. (If the pillow has a scalloped or shaped border of some type, it is best to allow the outside edge of the border to remain unfastened in order to show off the trim.) Pin or baste the knitted or crocheted pillow front in place. Turn the pillow over and sew the pillow front in place with small overcast stitches along the edge of the back side of the pillow, so that the stitches do not show on the front side.

Wall Hangings

In addition to the fabric mentioned in the instructions for your wall hanging, you will need sewing thread and needle or a sewing machine, small upholstery tacks, a dowel measuring the width of the wall hanging, and two hooks into which the dowel will fit snugly. Measure your finished crocheted or knitted wall hanging. From duck cloth, canvas, or the fabric specified in the instructions, cut a piece 2 inches larger all around than the wall hanging. Turn under 1 inch of the cloth twice all around and topstitch in place. Lay the wall hanging over the fabric with the wall hanging right side up and the fabric turnovers also facing up. Baste the wall hanging to the fabric around all four edges. Then, join the two pieces with rows of tacking stitches taken 6 inches apart across the entire wall hanging. Using upholstery tacks, tack the width of the top of the wall hanging to the dowel, placing the dowel just under the top edge. Insert or attach hooks to the wall, spacing them so that they are one-third of the width of the wall hanging apart, and rest the dowel on the hooks.

Rugs
Make the backing for rugs in the same manner as for wall hangings. In addition, you may want to pad the rug with cotton batting cut to size and inserted between the knitted or crocheted piece and the fabric backing. You may also want to outline the back of your rug with nonskid tape or double-faced tape to prevent its slipping on the floor.

METRIC CONVERSION TABLE

Linear Measure:
1 inch=2.54 centimeters
12 inches=1 foot=0.3048 meter
3 feet=1 yard=0.9144 meter
Square Measure:
1 square inch=6.4516 square centimeters
144 square inches=1 square foot=929.03 square centimeters
9 square feet=1 square yard=0.8361 square meter

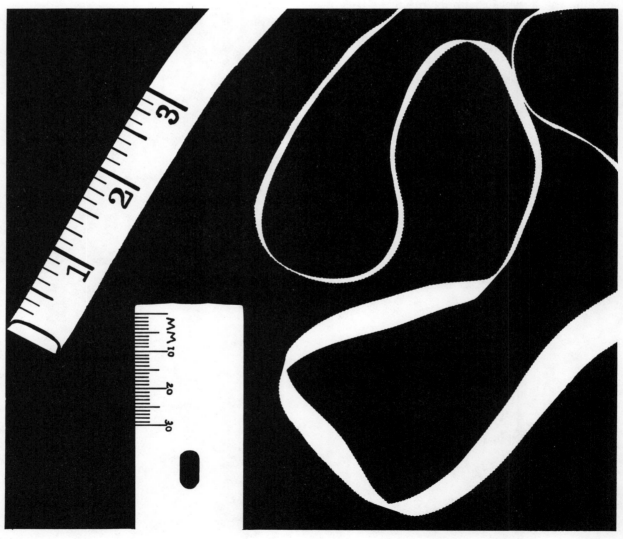

ABBREVIATIONS, SYMBOLS, AND TERMS

beg	begin, beginning
CC	contrasting color
ch	chain
ch-	(chain dash) refers to chain or space previously made, e.g., ch-1 sp
dc	double crochet
dec	decrease, decreases, decreased, decreasing
hdc	half double crochet
inc	increase, increases, increased, increasing
k	knit
lp(s)	loop(s)
MC	main color
p	purl
pat(s)	pattern(s)
psso	pass slip stitch(es) over [stitch(es)]
rnd(s)	round(s)
sc	single crochet
sl st	slip stitch
sp(s)	space(s)
st(s)	stitch(es)
tog	together
tr	triple (or treble) crochet
yo	yarn over
*or**	These symbols indicate that the directions immediately following are to be repeated a given number of times.
( )	Instructions within parentheses are to be repeated a given number of times.
Work even	Work without increasing or decreasing, always keeping pattern as established.

Simplified Instructions

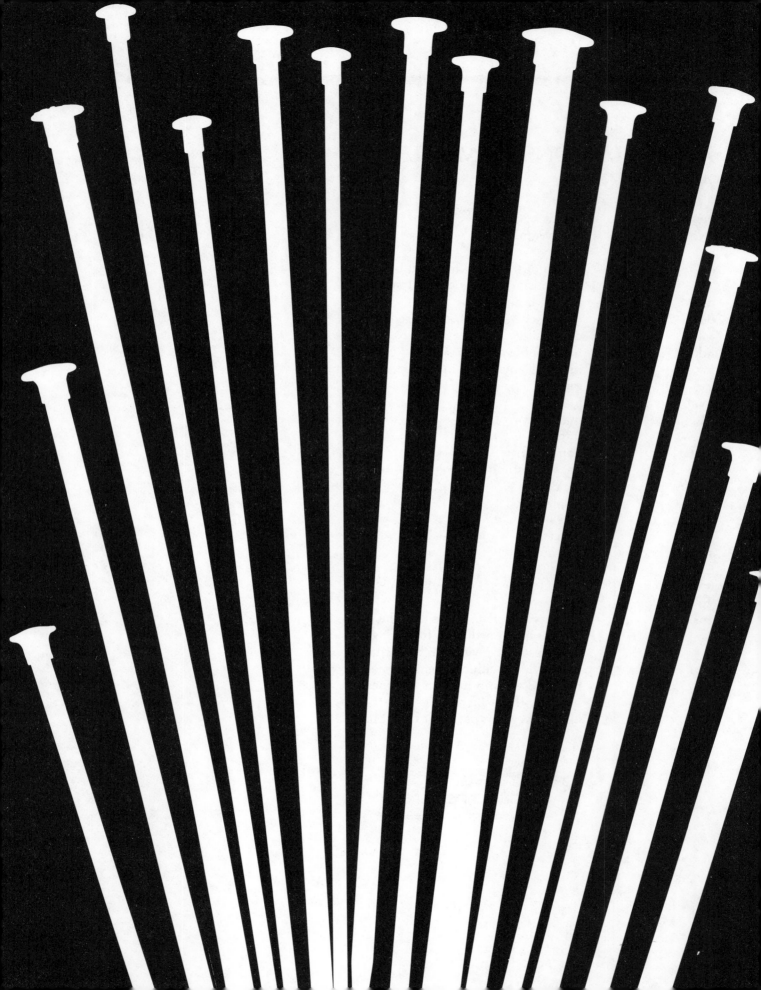

THE KNITTED HOME

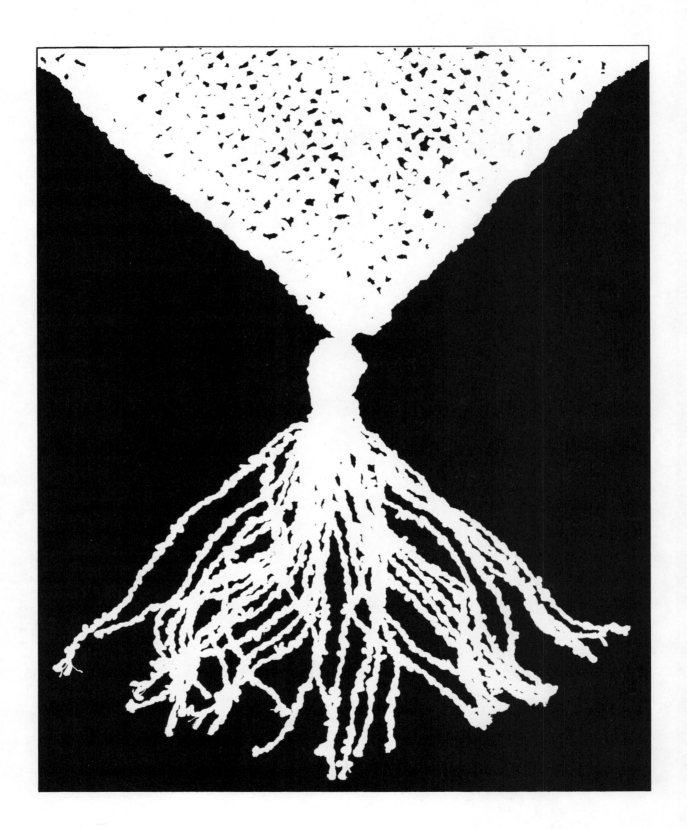

CONTEMPORARY LIVING ROOM

CHEVRON AFGHAN

Approximate finished size: 48 by 60 inches
No experience needed

A simple decrease stitch, worked at the center of every other row, shapes the strips of this light, airy afghan. Worked in brilliant tones, it will lend a summery accent to any room. The cotton-terry yarn adds texture to the easy stockinette-stitch pattern within the ability of even the beginner.

Materials:
Caron Cotton Terry, 50-gram (1.75-ounce) skeins
    8 skeins color 5011, mauve
    5 skeins color 5004, turquoise
    5 skeins color 5014, tangerine
Knitting needles, No. 8
Heavy-duty sewing thread

Gauge: 7 stitches=2 inches; 5 rows=1 inch

Strips: Make 3 in mauve, 2 in tangerine, and 2 in turquoise. For each strip, cast on 28 sts.
Row 1: Inc 1 st in first st, k 12, slip 1, k 2 tog, psso, k 11, inc 1 st in last st.
Row 2: Purl.
Repeat Rows 1 and 2 for pat until strip measures 60 inches along the center ridge, ending with a wrong-side row. Bind off.

Finishing: Using the heavy-duty thread and following the placement diagram, sew strips together.

Tassels: Make 3 in mauve, 2 in tangerine, and 2 in turquoise. For each tassel, cut fifteen 12-inch strands of yarn and tie a 6-inch strand around the middle. Fold the strands in half at the tie, wrap one end of one of the strands securely around the folded strands 3/4 inch below the tie, fasten off, and trim the ends evenly. Tie one tassel to each pointed end of a matching-color strip.

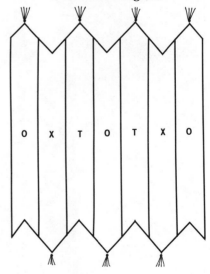

**Chevron Afghan
Placement Diagram**

Color Key
O=mauve
X=tangerine
T=turquoise

27

DIAGONALLY STRIPED PILLOWS

Approximate finished size: 13-inch square
Some experience needed

A set of three of these pillows, each with a different-colored stripe, would be a lovely accompaniment to the Chevron Afghan. Imagine them on a sofa of natural cotton or just tossed on a pine floor in a summer home. They would also be a comfy addition to your chaise lounge or to the cabin of your boat.

Materials:

Caron Cotton Terry, 50-gram (1.75-ounce) skeins
  For One Pillow:
  1 skein color 5002, natural
  1 skein color 5004, turquoise, or 1 skein color 5011, mauve
Knitting needles, No. 8
Two 15-inch squares of fabric
Polyester stuffing
Heavy-duty sewing thread

Gauge: 7 stitches=2 inches; 5 rows=1 inch

Note: When changing from one color and stitch section to another, be sure to work the first row of new color so that it appears as a knit row on the right side of the work. Notice that the pillow is worked on the diagonal.

Knitted Pillow Cover: With natural, cast on 3 sts. Work in stockinette st (k 1 row—right side; p 1 row—wrong side), inc 1 st at beg and end of every other row until there are 41 sts on needle; end wrong side. Change to turquoise or mauve and reverse stockinette st (p 1 row—right side; k 1 row—wrong side) and, starting with first row, continue to inc 1 st at beg and end of every other row until there are 55 sts on needle. Now, dec 1 st at beg and end of every other row until there are 41 sts on needle. Change to natural and stockinette st and dec 1 st at beg and end of every other row until there are 3 sts on needle. Bind off.

Finishing: Make a 13-inch-square pillow form from the fabric, following the general instructions at the beginning of the book. Sew the knitted pillow cover to pillow form.

CHAIR CUSHION

Approximate finished size: 13 inches at front edge
   tapering to 6 inches at back

Some experience needed

Our chair cushion is made for a straight-backed chair
and should increase your sitting comfort considerably
when padding a rush or cane seat. Make ties from fabric
matching the backing to secure the cushion in place.
You could make cushions for all your dining chairs, each
in a different shade of mauve, tangerine, or turquoise.

Materials:
Caron Cotton Terry, 50-gram (1.75-ounce) skeins
    For One Cushion:
    1 skein color 5002, natural
    1 skein color 5014, tangerine
Knitting needles, No. 8
Two 15-inch squares of fabric
Polyester stuffing or cotton batting
Heavy-duty sewing thread

Gauge: 7 stitches=2 inches; 5 rows=1 inch

Note: When changing from one color and stitch section to another, be sure to work the first row of new color so that it appears as a knit row on the right side of the work. Also, notice that the cushion is worked on the diagonal.

Knitted Cushion Cover: With natural, cast on 3 stitches. Work in stockinette st (k 1 row—right side; p 1 row—wrong side), inc 1 st at beg and end of every other row until there are 41 sts on needle, end wrong side. Change to tangerine and reverse stockinette st (p 1 row—right side; k 1 row—wrong side) and, beginning with first row, continue to inc 1 st every other row on left edge only, working even on right edge until there are 48 sts on needle, end wrong side. Now dec 1 st every other row at left edge only until there are 41 sts on needle, end wrong side. Change to natural and stockinette st and dec 1 st at beg and end of every other row until there are 27 sts on needle, end wrong side. Continue to dec 1 st on every other row on right edge 6 times and 1 st on every row on left edge 12 times until there are 9 sts left on needle; end wrong side. Bind off.

Finishing: Using the outline of the knitted cushion cover as a pattern (straighten piece first so that it lies symmetrically) and adding 1/2 inch all around for seam allowance, cut two pieces of fabric for the cushion form. With right sides of fabric facing, sew pieces together along two sides and front edge. Turn fabric right side out. Stuff with polyester stuffing or cotton batting cut to fit. Sew remaining side closed with slip stitches, turning in seam allowance. Sew knitted cushion cover to top of pillow form, using an overcast stitch.

STRIPED RUG

Approximate finished size: 28 by 38 inches
No experience needed

The final project for our contemporary living room is
this multicolor, fringed throw rug, beautiful on a
scrubbed wood floor or brick tile. Backing the rug with
heavy fabric will add some body to the lightweight piece.

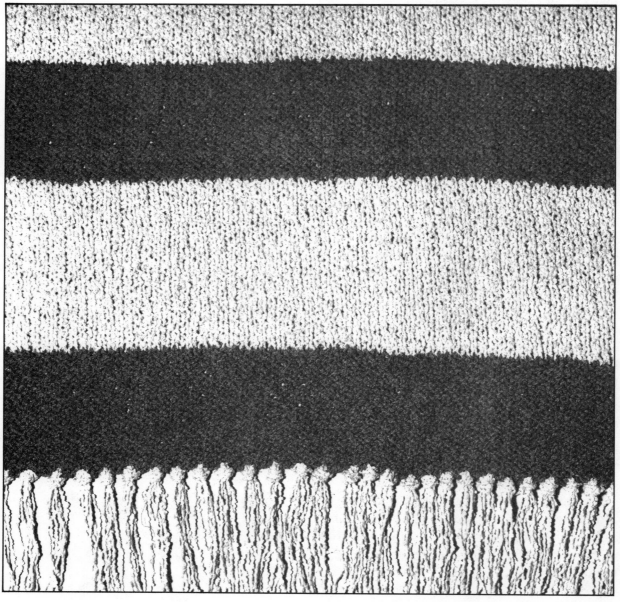

Materials:

Caron Cotton Terry, 50-gram (1.75-ounce) skeins

    5 skeins color 5002, natural
    2 skeins color 5014, tangerine
    2 skeins color 5004, turquoise
    1 skein color 5011, mauve

Knitting needles, No. 8

One 30- by 45-inch piece of fabric

Heavy-duty sewing thread

Gauge: 7 stitches=2 inches; 5 rows=1 inch

Note: When changing from one color and stitch section to another, be sure to work the first row of new color so that it appears as a knit row on the right side of the work.

Knitted Rug: With turquoise, cast on 98 sts. Work even in reverse stockinette st (p 1 row—right side; k 1 row—wrong side) for 18 rows. Change to natural and stockinette st (k 1 row—right side; p 1 row—wrong side) and work even for 26 rows. Continue to alternate 18 rows of reverse stockinette st with 26 rows stockinette st in color order as follows: tangerine, mauve, tangerine, and turquoise. Bind off.

Fringe: Cut 8-inch lengths of yarn in natural and knot 3 strands in every fourth st along each short edge of rug.

Finishing: Make a rug backing from the fabric, following the general instructions at the beginning of the book. Sew the knitted rug to the backing.

ENGLISH COUNTRY BEDROOM

ROSE-EMBROIDERED AFGHAN

Approximate finished size: 45½ by 60 inches
No experience needed

Cabbage roses, inspired by the flowered chintz typically used on furniture in an English country home, have been embroidered with duplicate stitch on a background of creamy white stockinette-stitch knitting. The dusty rose tones of the flower contrast with the green of the leaves to produce a most romantic look.

Materials:
Lion Brand Sayelle, 100-gram (3.5-ounce) skeins
    10 skeins color 99, eggshell
      1 skein color 104, blush
      1 skein color 141, dusty rose
      1 skein color 175, sage
Knitting needles, No. 7
Yarn needle

Gauge in Stockinette Stitch: 19 stitches＝4 inches;
7 rows＝1 inch

Seed Stitch:
Row 1: *K 1, p 1, repeat from * across, ending with k 1
only if there are an uneven number of sts.
Row 2: P the k sts, k the p sts.
Repeat Row 2 for pat st.

Center Panel: With eggshell, cast on 70 sts. Work in
seed st for 10 rows. *Change to stockinette st (k 1
row—right side; p 1 row—wrong side) on center 64 sts,
continuing to work first 3 and last 3 sts in seed st. Work
even in this manner for 13¼ inches, end wrong side.
Change to seed st on all sts and work even for 10 rows.
Repeat from * 3 times more. Bind off in seed st.

Right Panel: With eggshell, cast on 73 sts. Work in seed
st for 10 rows. *Change to stockinette st on center
64 sts, keeping first 6 (right-edge) and last 3 (left-edge)
sts in seed st. Work even in this manner for 13¼ inches,
end wrong side. Change to seed st on all sts and work even
for 10 rows. Repeat from * 3 times more. Bind off in seed st.

Left Panel: Work as for right panel, but keep first 3
(right-edge) and last 6 (left-edge) sts in seed st while
working stockinette st on center sts.

Embroidery: With yarn needle and blush, dusty rose,
and sage yarns, follow chart to embroider duplicate-
stitch rose, centering design on first and third
stockinette-stitch squares of right and left panels and on
second and fourth squares of center panel.

Finishing: Block panels lightly. With right and left
panels in proper position, sew panels together with yarn
needle and yarn.

Rose-Embroidered Afghan Chart

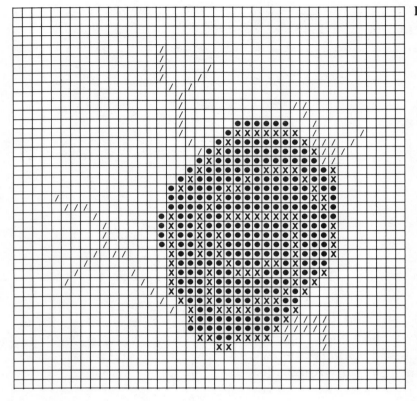

Color Key
X = dusty rose
● = blush
/ = sage green

38

ROSE-EMBROIDERED PILLOW

Approximate finished size: 16-inch square
No experience needed

Duplicate stitch is simple and enjoyable to work. Once
you've gotten the general idea of the flower design,
you'll probably be able to work the flower free-hand.
Put in the darker tones first and then fill in the lighter
areas of blush. Several pillows, each embroidered with a
slightly different flower, would produce a nice effect.

Materials:
Lion Brand Sayelle, 100-gram (3.5-ounce) skeins
    1 skein color 99, eggshell
    1 skein color 104, blush
    1 skein color 141, dusty rose
    1 skein color 175, sage
Knitting needles, No. 7
Yarn needle
Two 18-inch squares of fabric
Polyester stuffing
Sewing thread

Gauge in Stockinette Stitch: 19 stitches=4 inches;
7 rows=1 inch

Seed Stitch:
Row 1: *K 1, p 1, repeat from * across, end k 1 if there
is an uneven number of sts.
Row 2: P the k sts, k the p sts.
Repeat Row 2 for pat st.

Pillow Cover: With eggshell, cast on 76 sts. Work in
seed st for 10 rows. Change to stockinette st (k 1
row—right side; p 1 row—wrong side) on center 64 sts,
continuing to work first and last 6 sts in seed st. Work
even in this manner for 13¼ inches. Change to seed st
on all 76 sts and work even for 10 rows. Bind off in
seed st.

Embroidery: With blush, dusty rose, and sage yarns,
follow chart to embroider duplicate-stitch rose, centering
design on stockinette-stitch portion of knitted square.

Finishing: Block lightly. Make a 15½-inch-square pillow
form from fabric, following the general instructions at
the beginning of the book. Sew knitted pillow cover to
pillow form.

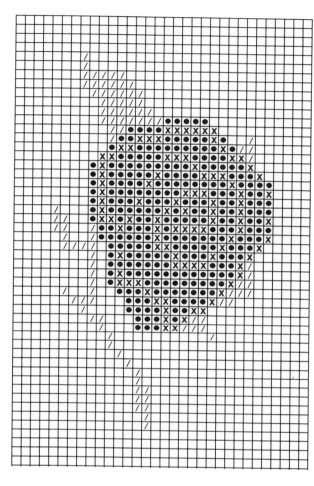

Rose-Embroidered Pillow Chart

Color Key
X = dusty rose
● = blush
/ = sage green

Rose-Embroidered Footstool Cover Chart

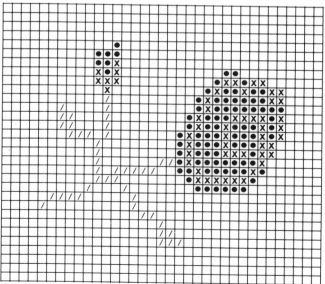

ROSE-EMBROIDERED FOOTSTOOL COVER

Approximate finished size: 17 by 22½ inches
No experience needed

Just about everyone has a battered footstool that needs to
be recovered. Why not add this project to your cabbage
rose afghan and pillow? General instructions for making a
piece to cover the dimensions of your footstool are
included. The duplicate-stitch design on this cover is a deli-
cate bud but you could always "paint" an entire bouquet.

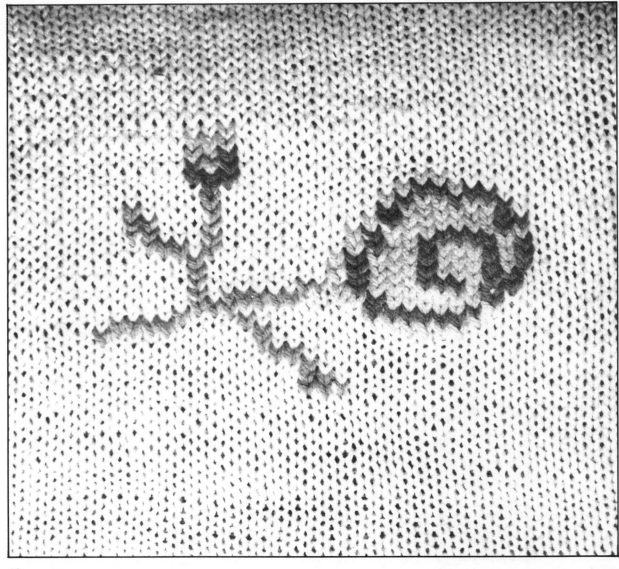

Materials:
Lion Brand Sayelle, 100-gram (3.5-ounce) skeins
    1 skein color 99, eggshell
    1 skein color 104, blush
    1 skein color 141, dusty rose
    1 skein color 175, sage
Knitting needles, No. 7
Yarn needle
Enough of 3/4-inch-wide twisted braid to go around
    footstool
Sewing thread to match braid

Gauge: 19 stitches=4 inches; 7 rows=1 inch

Note: To change the size of this piece to fit your own footstool, cover it with a piece of fabric, pleating the corners for a good fit, and then measure the fabric. Then, simply make the knitted piece to that size.

Footstool Cover: With eggshell, cast on 106 sts. Work even in stockinette st (k 1 row—right side; p 1 row—wrong side) for 17 inches. Bind off.

Embroidery: With blush, dusty rose, and sage yarns, follow chart to embroider duplicate-stitch rose, centering design on knitted rectangle.

Finishing: Block lightly. Center embroidered area of piece on footstool, folding and tucking corners of the remainder to fit. Sew braid around bottom edge of knitted piece.

Rose-Embroidered Footstool Cover chart on page 41.

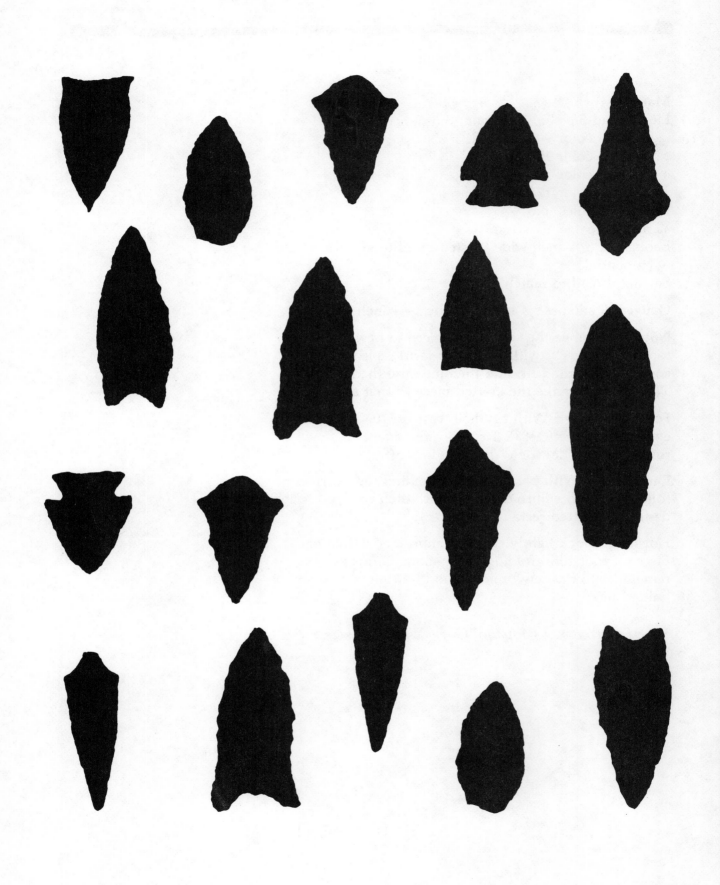

SOUTHWESTERN ROOM
FOR A BOY

ARROWHEAD AFGHAN

Approximate finished size: 40 by 52 inches
Some experience needed

The masculine tone of this Arrowhead Afghan, worked in strips of positive/negative reverse design, sets the tone for this Southwestern room for a boy but would look equally fine in any man's study or den. Use a separate bobbin for each arrow to avoid having to carry yarn across the back of the work.

Materials:
Caron Wintuk-4 Hand Knitting Yarn, 85-gram (3-ounce) balls
  5 balls color 39, wood rose
  4 balls color 160, oxford heather
Knitting needles, No. 7
Crochet hook, size G

Gauge: 9 stitches = 2 inches; 13 rows = 2 inches

Note: The use of bobbins is recommended.

Wood Rose Strips: Make 3. With wood rose, cast on 36 sts. Work in stockinette st (k 1 row—right side; p 1 row—wrong side), following chart for color changes and working arrow design in oxford heather. Work from A to B 8 times, and from A to C once. Bind off.

Oxford Heather Strips: Make 2. With oxford heather, cast on 36 sts. Work as for wood rose strips, reversing colors.

Finishing: Sew strips together, alternating wood rose and oxford heather strips. Work 1 row of color-over-color single crochet around joined piece, working 3 single crochet in each corner.

Fringe: Work color-over-color fringe on short end of each strip. Cut 8-inch lengths of yarn and knot 3 strands in every fourth st.

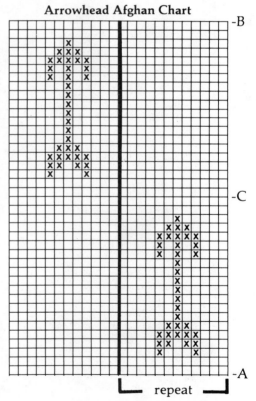

Arrowhead Afghan Chart

Color Key
□ = wood rose or oxford heather
X = oxford heather or wood rose

INDIAN RUG

Approximate finished size: 24 by 36 inches
Experience needed

Our rug is inspired partly by a pattern from Navajo
weaving called the butterfly design. These are the shapes
you find in the four corners of this fringed rug. An old
blanket will make a perfect backing fabric for it.

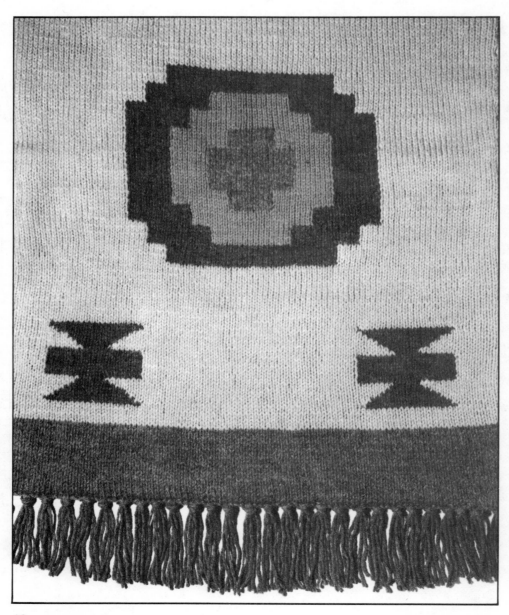

Materials:
Caron Wintuk-4 Hand Knitting Yarn, 85-gram (3-ounce) balls
    3 balls color 17, fawn
    2 balls color 163, brown heather
    1 ball color 160, oxford heather
    1 ball color 39, wood rose
Knitting needles, No. 8
Crochet hook, size G
One 26- by 36-inch piece of fabric
Sewing thread

Gauge: 4 stitches=1 inch; 11 rows=2 inches

Note: The use of bobbins is recommended.

Rug: With brown heather, cast on 96 sts. Work in stockinette st (k 1 row—right side; p 1 row—wrong side) for 22 rows. Then work the chart in stockinette st, following it for color changes. Only the lower right-hand quarter of chart is shown. To work the complete chart, work sts of each row across from A to B and then back from B to A. Then work rows from A to C and back from C to A. Work 22 more rows stockinette st with brown heather and bind off.

Finishing: Work 1 row of color-over-color sc around piece, working 3 sc in each corner. Block piece.

Fringe: Cut 8-inch lengths of brown heather. Knot 3 strands in every fourth stitch along short edges of rug. Back the rug with fabric, following the general instructions at the beginning of the book.

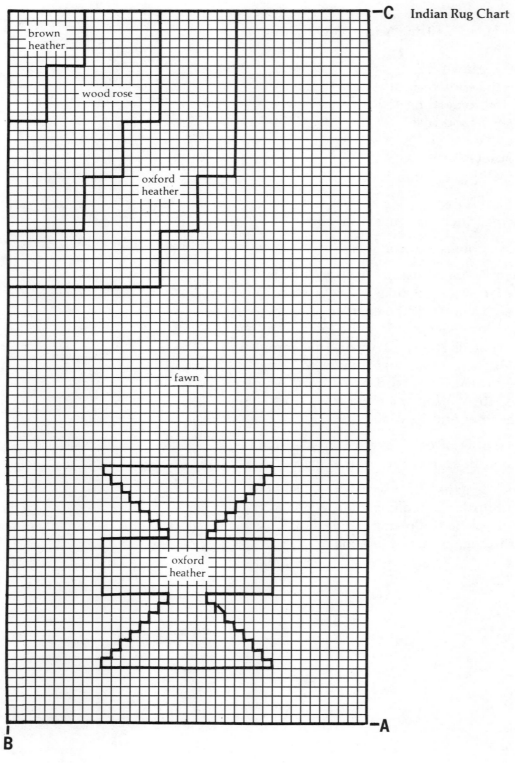

C — **Indian Rug Chart**

brown heather

wood rose

oxford heather

fawn

oxford heather

—A

B

INDIAN WALL HANGING

Approximate finished size: 30-inch square
Experience needed

The wall hanging in our set of designs from the old
Southwest is based on the butterfly design from Navajo
weaving mentioned in the Indian Rug project. The
butterfly shapes are interlocked here, worked in
contrasting earth tones at the center of the piece. Back
the hanging with a piece of heavy material.

Materials:

Caron Wintuk-4 Hand Knitting Yarn, 85-gram (3.5-ounce) balls

  2 balls color 163, brown heather
  2 balls color 17, fawn
  1 ball color 39, wood rose
  1 ball color 160, oxford heather

Knitting needles, No. 8

Crochet hook, size G

One 32-inch piece of fabric

Sewing thread

30-inch piece of wood doweling

Gauge: 4 stitches=1 inch; 11 rows=2 inches

Note: The use of bobbins is recommended.

Wall Hanging: With brown heather, cast on 120 sts. Work in stockinette st (k 1 row—right side; p 1 row—wrong side) for 22 rows. Then work the chart in stockinette st, following it for color changes. Only the right-hand quarter of chart is shown. To work complete chart, work sts of each row across from A to B and then back from B to A. Then work rows from A to C and then back from C to A. Work 22 more rows stockinette st with brown heather and bind off.

Finishing: Work 1 row of color-over-color sc around finished piece, working 3 sc in each corner. Make backing from fabric and mount wall hanging, following general instructions at the beginning of the book.

Indian Wall Hanging Chart

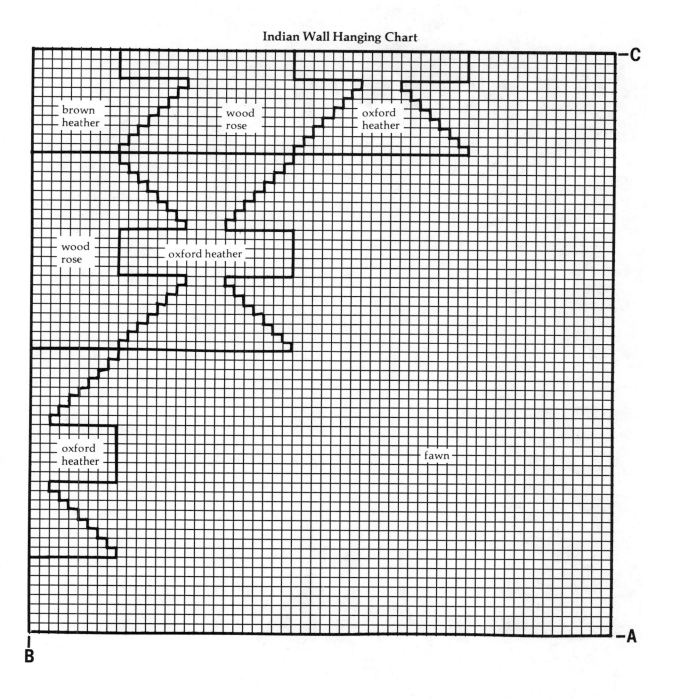

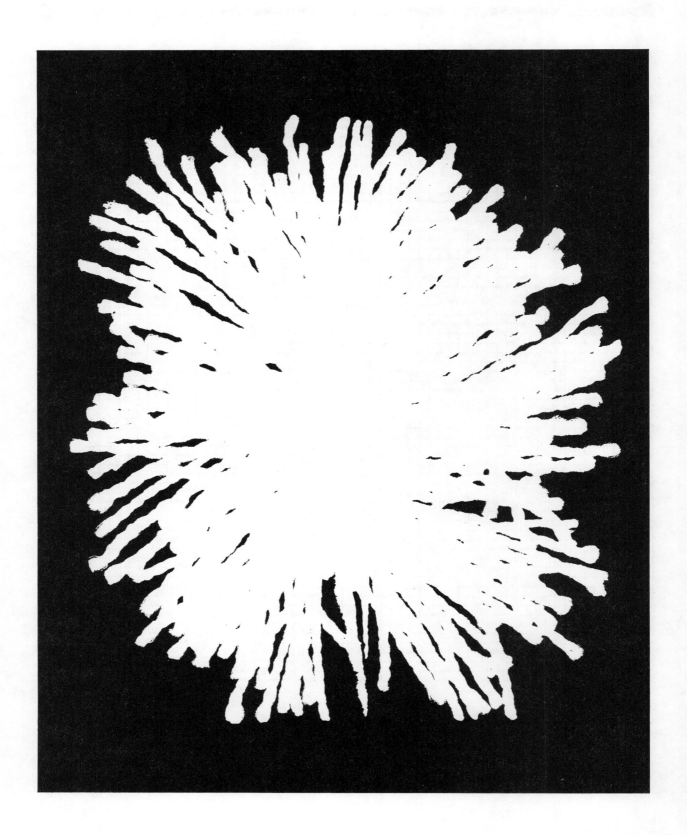

ABSTRACT PRIMARY COLORS
FOR A GIRL'S ROOM

ABSTRACT AFGHAN

Approximate finished size: 38 by 51 inches

No experience needed

Bold splashes of color are thrown against a pure white
canvas of stockinette-stitch to create a lively afghan for
the modern girl. The fringes are knotted through triangular-
shaped areas of yarn-over mesh knitted into the overall
stockinette-stitch pattern.

Materials:

Coats & Clark Red Heart Bulky, 85-gram (3-ounce) skeins

    12 skeins color 1, white

     3 skeins color 902, jockey red

     3 skeins color 848, skipper blue

     3 skeins color 230, yellow

     3 skeins color 676, emerald

Knitting needles, No. 10

Crochet hook, size K

Gauge in Stockinette Stitch: 7 stitches=2 inches;
5 rows=1 inch

Note: Afghan is made in one piece.

Afghan: With jockey red, cast on 130 sts. Work even in garter st (k every row) for 8 rows. Continue to work 3 more stripes of 8-row garter st, changing color first to emerald, then yellow, and finally skipper blue. Change to white and stockinette st (k 1 row—right side; p 1 row—wrong side) and follow chart for stitch changes. Work sts of each row from A to B once, from B to C 3 times, and from C to D once. Work rows from A to E one time, from F to E 2 times, and from F to G one time. Bind off.

Finishing: With crochet hook and jockey red, work 2 rows sc around white stockinette portion of afghan, working 3 sc in each corner. Block.

Fringe: Cut 6-inch strands of jockey red, yellow, skipper blue, and emerald. With crochet hook, knot 3 strands in each yarn-over stitch on afghan, alternating colors as you please.

Abstract Afghan Chart

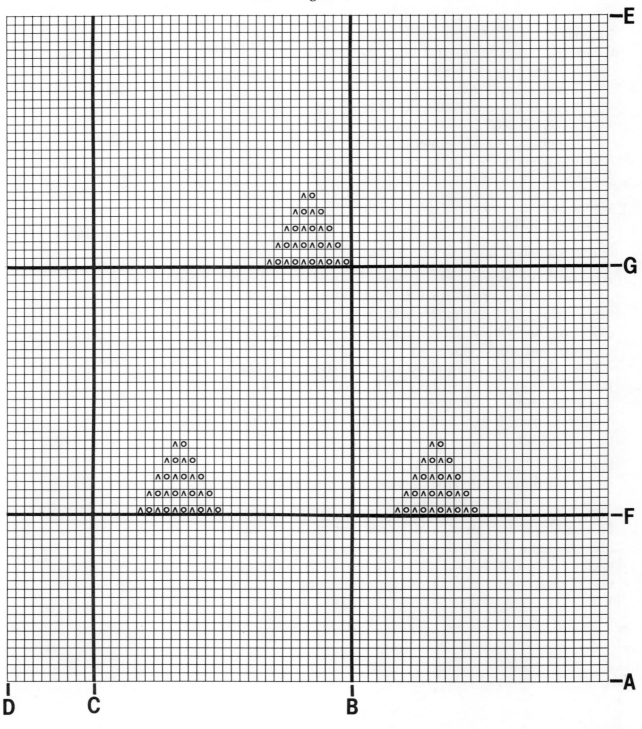

Stitch Key
O = yo
Λ = k 2 tog

SHAGGY PILLOW

Approximate finished size: 14 by 15½ inches
No experience needed

Made with bulky yarn, this simple pillow is a good
beginner's project. It's quick and easy and the perfect
partner for the Abstract Afghan. A bright fabric could
be used in making the pillow form to jazz it up even
more. Another idea would be to make several pillows,
each white with only one contrasting color per pillow.

Materials:
Coats & Clark Red Heart Bulky, 85-gram (3-ounce) skeins
   1 skein color 1, white
   1 skein color 902, jockey red
   1 skein color 848, skipper blue
   1 skein color 230, yellow
   1 skein color 676, emerald
Knitting needles, No. 10
Crochet hook, size K
Two pieces 16- by 17½-inch fabric
Sewing thread
Polyester stuffing

Gauge in Stockinette Stitch: 7 stitches=2 inches;
5 rows=1 inch

Pillow Cover: With jockey red, cast on 50 sts. Work even in garter st (k every row) for 8 rows. Continue to work 3 more stripes of 8-row garter st, changing color first to emerald, then yellow, and finally skipper blue. Change to white and stockinette st (k 1 row—right side; p 1 row—wrong side) and follow chart for stitch changes. Bind off.

Fringe: Cut 6-inch strands of jockey red, yellow, skipper blue, and emerald. With crochet hook, knot 3 strands in each yarn-over stitch on afghan, alternating colors as you please.

Finishing: With crochet hook and jockey red, work 2 rows sc around white stockinette portion of afghan, working 3 sc in each corner. Block. Make a 14- by 15½-inch pillow form from fabric, following the general instructions at the beginning of the book. Sew knitted pillow cover to pillow form.

Shaggy Pillow Chart

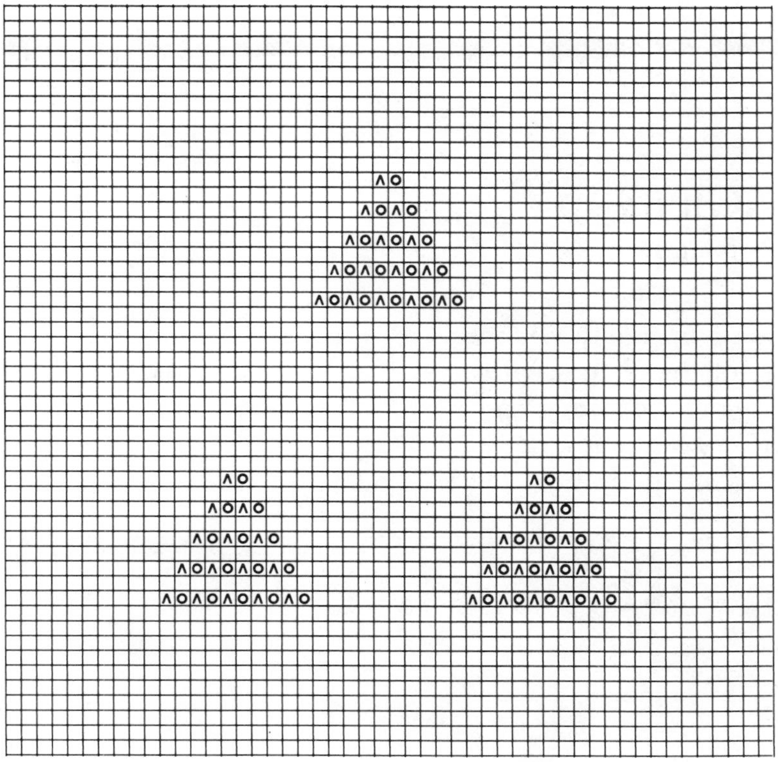

Stitch Key
O = yo
Λ = k 2 tog

Splashy Wall Hanging Chart

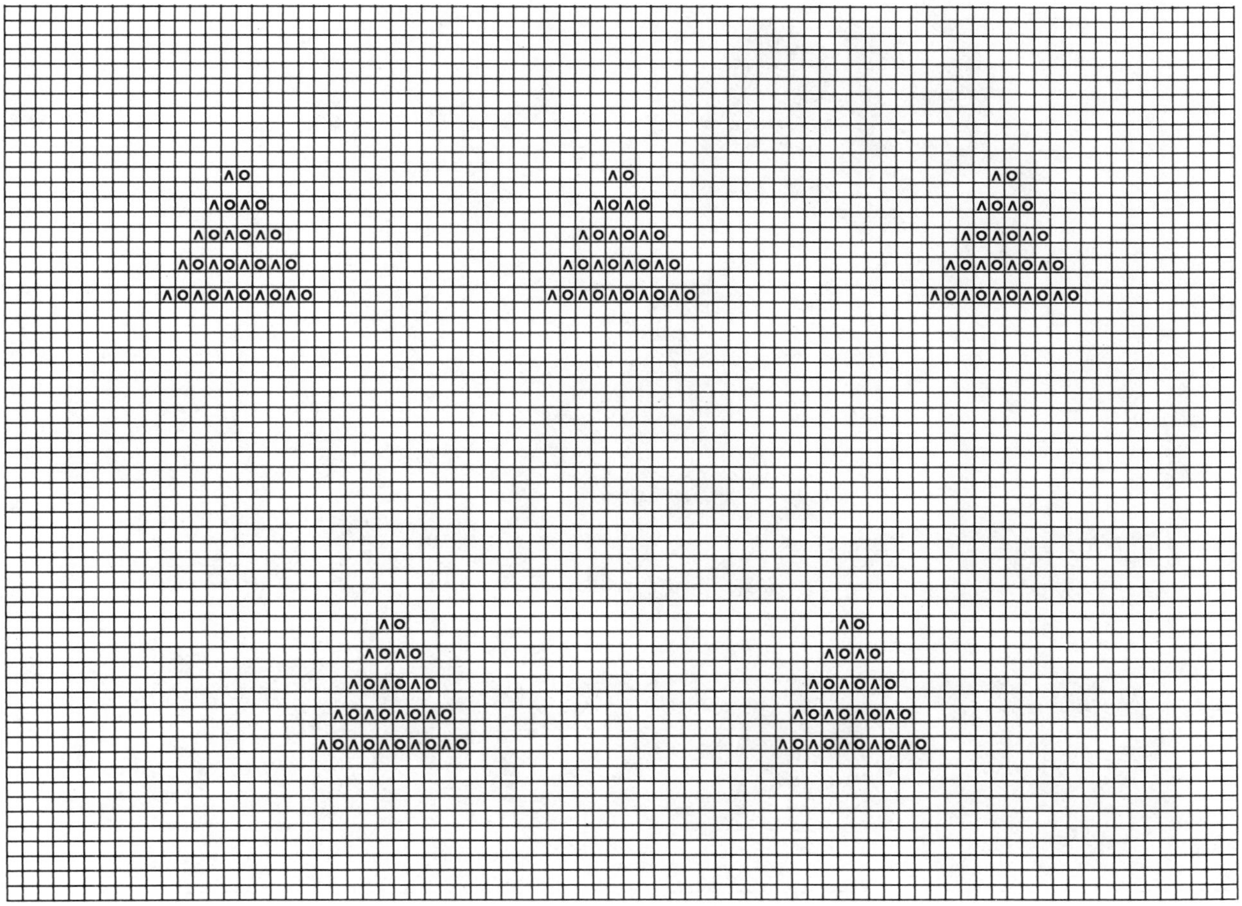

SPLASHY WALL HANGING

Approximate finished size: 24 by 29 inches

No experience needed

This project can be hung sideways or upside down and still look terrific. Just be sure to knot the fringes with the piece in the same position that it will be hung. A piece of heavy-weight fabric, such as blanketing or rug canvas, should be used to give body to the knitted piece.

Materials:
Coats & Clark Red Heart Bulky, 85-gram (3-ounce) skeins
    2 skeins color 1, white
    1 skein color 902, jockey red
    1 skein color 848, skipper blue
    1 skein color 230, yellow
    1 skein color 676, emerald
Knitting needles, No. 10
Crochet hook, size K
One piece 26- by 31-inch fabric
Sewing thread

Gauge in Stockinette Stitch: 7 stitches=2 inches;
5 rows=1 inch

Wall Hanging: With jockey red, cast on 80 sts. Work even in garter st (k every row) for 8 rows. Continue to work 3 more stripes of 8-row garter st, changing color first to emeràld, then yellow, and finally skipper blue. Change to white and stockinette st (k 1 row—right side; p 1 row—wrong side) and follow chart for stitch changes, working rows from A to B 2 times. Bind off.

Fringe: Cut 6-inch strands of jockey red, yellow, skipper blue, and emerald. With crochet hook, knot 3 strands in each yarn-over stitch on afghan, alternating colors as you please.

Finishing: With crochet hook and jockey red, work 2 rows sc around white stockinette portion of afghan, working 3 sc in each corner. Block. Make backing from fabric and mount wall hanging, following general instructions in the beginning of the book.

Splashy Wall Hanging chart on page 61.

CONTEMPORARY LIVING ROOM: Chevron Afghan, p. 26; Diagonally Striped Pillow, p. 28; Striped Rug, p. 32.

KNITTED PROJECTS FOR ON-THE-GO:
(right) Portable Plaid Lap Robe, p. 78;
Striped Shawl, p. 82; Striped Travel
Pillow, p. 84.
SOUTHWESTERN ROOM FOR A BOY:
(below) Arrowhead Afghan, p. 46; Indian
Rug, p. 48; Indian Wall Hanging, p. 51.

PREPPY PLAIDS FOR A BOY'S ROOM:
(above) Blue Plaid Lap Robe, p. 108;
Blue Plaid Pillow, p. 110; Hassock
Cover, p. 112.
CROCHETED PROJECTS FOR ON-THE-GO:
(right) Bargello Lap Robe, p. 142;
Bargello Shawl, p. 144; Bargello
Travel Pillow, p. 146.

DECO MASTER BEDROOM: (left)
Ripple Afghan, p. 100; Textured
Pillow, p. 102; Filet Mesh Rug,
p. 105.
POCKET ANIMAL NURSERY:
(below) Pocket Animal Baby
Blanket, p. 129; Pocket Animal
Pillow, p. 134; Beribboned Diaper
Storage Bag, p. 137.

FRENCH PROVINCIAL LIVING ROOM: Flowered Lap Robe, p. 89; Filet Mesh Pillow, p. 91; Lacy Round Pillow, p. 94; Ruffled Doily, p. 97.

CONTEMPORARY NURSERY

APPLE BABY BLANKET

Approximate finished size: 32 by 40 inches
Experience needed

Pinstripes of red, white, and blue streak across the alphabet-bordered baby blanket for the contemporary nursery. The border is the only challenging aspect of this project; the use of bobbins is recommended. Otherwise the pattern is quite easy. The "apple" and "A" design could be worked in duplicate stitch instead of being knitted in, if desired.

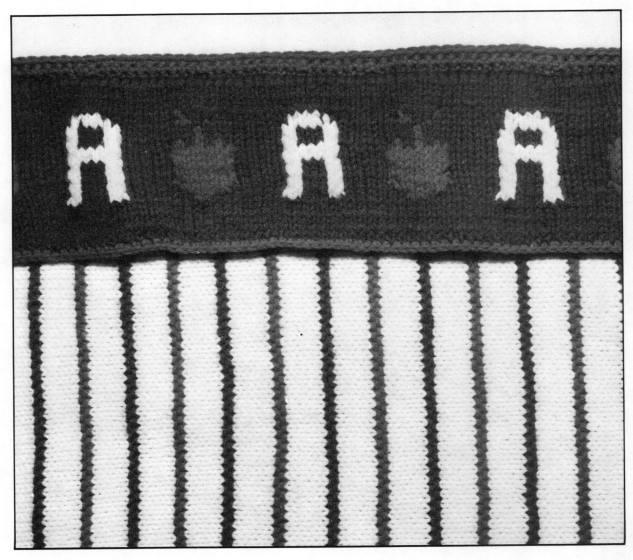

Materials:
Brunswick Windrush (100% Orlon Acrylic from Dupont),
100-gram (3.5-ounce) skeins
    3 skeins color 90100, ecru
    1 skein color 9012, royal
    1 skein color 1025, bright scarlet
Knitting needles, No. 8
Crochet hook, size G

Gauge in Stockinette Stitch: 4 stitches=1 inch;
6 rows=1 inch

Pattern Stitch:
Rows 1 through 6: With ecru, work in stockinette st
(k 1 row—right side; p 1 row—wrong side).
Rows 7 and 8: With bright scarlet, k.
Repeat Rows 1 through 8 for pat st, alternating bright
scarlet stripes with royal.

Blanket: With ecru, cast on 160 sts. Work in pat st until
12 bright scarlet stripes and 11 royal stripes have been
completed. Work Rows 1 through 6 once more. Bind
off loosely.

Border: With royal, cast on 125 sts. Work in stockinette
st (k 1 row—right side; p 1 row—wrong side), following
chart to completion. Bind off loosely.

Finishing: With right side of border facing, crochet
hook, and bright scarlet yarn, and working across cast-
on edge of border only, single crochet evenly across,
working 3 single crochet to every 4 stitches. Fasten off.
Baste border over one short edge of blanket. (Note that
the top edge is a double thickness when the border is in
place.) Baste sides of border to sides of blanket. *Edging:*
Rnd 1: With right side facing, crochet hook, and bright
scarlet yarn, sc evenly around entire blanket, working
through a double thickness at the top border edges,
working about 3 sc to every 4 sts of knit, and working
3 sc in each corner. Join with a sl st to first sc. Turn.
Rnd 2: With wrong side facing, work 1 sc in each sc
around, working 3 sc in each corner. Join with sl st to
first sc. Turn. *Rnd 3:* With right side facing, work 1 sc
in each sc around, working 3 sc in each corner.
Block lightly.

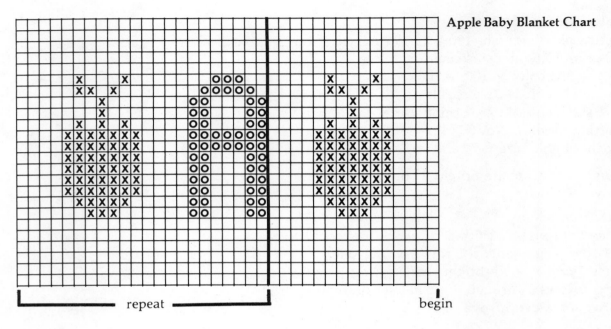

Apple Baby Blanket Chart

repeat ━━━   begin

Color Key
□ = royal
X = bright scarlet
O = ecru

APPLE SHELF EDGING

Approximate finished size: 31 by 3½ inches
Experience needed

The shelf edging in our contemporary nursery is an
encore of the border design on the Apple Baby Blanket.
The strip can be made to any size and, if desired, be
backed to add more stability. As for the blanket, the
strips can be made in solid blue and the designs
embroidered in duplicate stitch afterwards.

Materials:
Brunswick Windrush (100% Orlon Acrylic from Dupont),
100-gram (3.5-ounce) skeins
    1 skein color 9012, royal
    1 skein color 1025, bright scarlet
Knitting needles, No. 8
Crochet hook, size G

Gauge: 4 stitches=1 inch; 6 rows=1 inch

Note: Shelf edging may be made longer by adding more repeats; each repeat is 22 sts (5½ inches) long. Yarn amount given is sufficient for two strips of edging.

Shelf Edging: With royal, cast on 125 sts. Work in stockinette st (k 1 row—right side; p 1 row—wrong side), following chart to completion. Bind off loosely. *Edging:* With right side of border facing crochet hook and bright scarlet yarn, work 1 row of sc evenly spaced around piece, working 3 sc to every 4 sts and 3 sc in each corner. Fasten off.

Finishing: Attach edging to shelf with double-stick tape or strips of Velcro sewn to shelf edging and the matching strips of Velcro glued to the shelf.

Apple Shelf Edging Chart

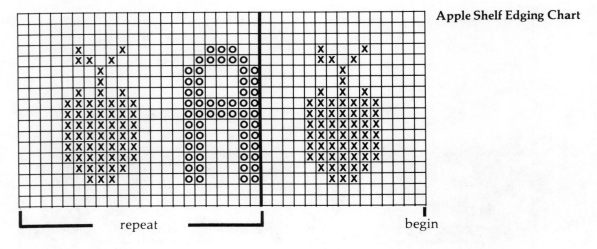

repeat   begin

Color Key
□ =royal
X =bright scarlet
O =ecru

70

SOFT BLOCKS

Approximate finished size: 5½-inch cubes
Some experience needed

It's "apples" and "A's" again on our soft blocks, which are fun to throw around and they're so cuddly no one will get hurt. The squares that make up the block are perfect carry-along work. You might like to design your own "B/Ball" blocks and "C/Cat" blocks to carry out the theme.

Materials:
Brunswick Windrush (100% Orlon Acrylic from Dupont), 100-gram (3.5-ounce) skeins
    1 skein color 9012, royal
    1 skein color 1025, bright scarlet
    1 skein color 90100, ecru
Knitting needles, No. 8
Crochet hook, size K
Polyester stuffing

Gauge: 4 stitches=1 inch; 6 rows=1 inch

Note: The two pillow blocks are identical, each being made of six equal sections. The top section is bright scarlet, the bottom royal; each side section shows an apple or the letter A. The yarn amount given is sufficient for two blocks.

Top Section: Make 1 for each block. With bright scarlet, cast on 24 sts. Work even in stockinette st (k 1 row—right side; p 1 row—wrong side) for 36 rows. Bind off loosely.

Bottom Section: Make 1 for each block. With royal, cast on 24 sts. Work in stockinette st as for top section.

Apple Side Section: Make 2 for each block. With royal, cast on 24 sts. Work even in stockinette st, following chart A to completion. Bind off loosely.

Letter Side Section: Make 2 for each block. With royal, cast on 24 sts. Work even in stockinette st, following chart B to completion. Bind off loosely.

Finishing: For each block, with right sides facing, sew the 4 side pieces together, alternating letter and apple sections. With right sides still facing, sew bright scarlet section to top and royal section to bottom along 3 sides only. Turn to right side. Stuff block firmly and overcast last side closed.

Trim: With crochet hook and 2 strands of bright scarlet held together, make a chain about 5¾ inches long, or long enough to cover one seam, and sew in place. In this manner, make 11 more chains for each block and sew securely in place to cover each seam.

Soft Block Charts

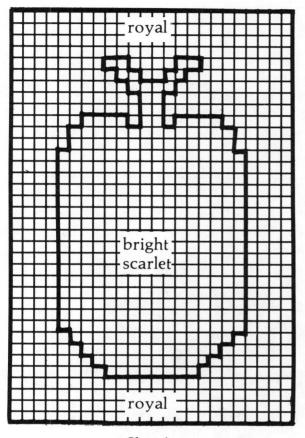

Chart A

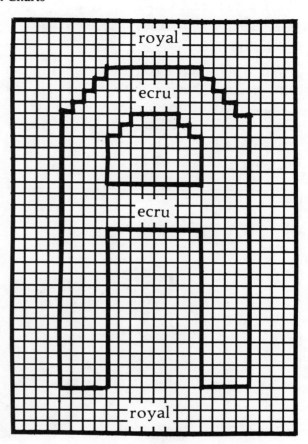

Chart B

73

APPLE PILLOW

Approximate finished size: 11-inch square
Some experience needed

A small, flat pillow is the only appropriate kind for a little one and this is baby's first! A big, red, knitted-in apple is recognizable to the youngest toddler and coordinates with the other projects in the contemporary nursery. Make the pillow form in a bright red to carry out the color scheme.

Materials:
Brunswick Windrush (100% Orlon Acrylic from Dupont),
100-gram (3.5-ounce) skeins
    1 skein color 9012, royal
    1 skein color 1025, bright scarlet
Knitting needles, No. 8
Crochet hook, size G
Two 13-inch squares of fabric
Sewing thread
Polyester stuffing

Gauge: 4 stitches=1 inch; 6 rows=1 inch

Pillow: With royal, cast on 45 sts. Work even in
stockinette st (k 1 row—right side; p 1 row—wrong
side) and follow chart to completion. Bind off.

Finishing: With crochet hook and royal, sc evenly
around knitted piece, working 3 sc in each corner. Join
with sl st to first sc. Fasten off. Make an 11½-inch-
square pillow form from fabric, following the general
instructions at the beginning of the book. Sew knitted
pillow cover to pillow form.

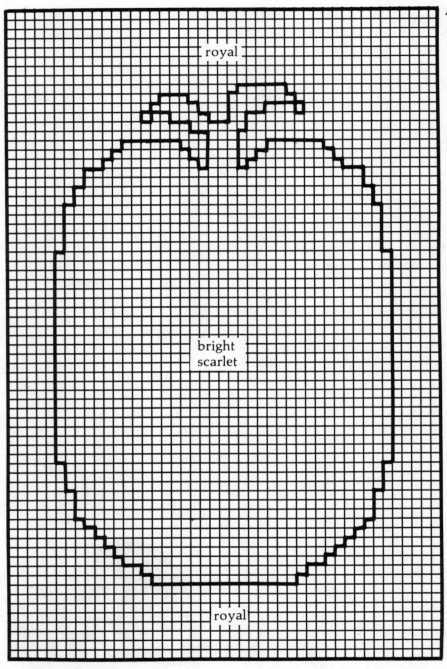

royal

bright
scarlet

royal

76

KNITTED PROJECTS
FOR ON-THE-GO

PORTABLE PLAID LAP ROBE

Approximate finished size: 40 by 50 inches, unfolded
Some experience needed

Designed to take the comforts of home along for travel
of any kind, whether by air, by land, or by sea, this lap
robe folds into a handy carrying bag with braided
handles. Keep it in the car at all times for naps in the
back seat or for trips to football games.

Materials:
Caron Rug and Craft Yarn, 1.6-ounce (70-yard) skeins
    9 skeins color 0013, brick
    6 skeins color 0012, burnt orange
    3 skeins color 002, creme
Knitting needles, No. 10½
Crochet hooks, sizes J and K
Two large buttons

Gauge: 3 stitches = 1 inch; 4 rows = 1 inch

Note: The use of bobbins is recommended.

Center Strip: With brick, cast on 10 sts, followed by 6 sts creme, 28 sts brick, 6 sts creme, and 10 sts brick—60 sts. Work even in stockinette st (k 1 row—right side; p 1 row—wrong side), working chart for Center Strip from A to B one time and then from B to C 8 times; end by working from C to D once. Bind off.

Right Strip: With brick, cast on 14 sts, followed by 6 sts creme and 10 sts brick—30 sts. Work even in stockinette st, working chart for right strip from A to B once and then from B to C 8 times; end by working from C to D once. Bind off.

Left Strip: With brick, cast on 10 sts, followed by 6 sts creme and 14 sts brick—30 sts. Work even in stockinette st, working chart for left strip from A to B once and then from B to C 8 times; end by working from C to D once. Bind off.

Finishing: With J crochet hook and burnt orange, join center strip to side strips as follows. Holding center strip toward you and with wrong sides of center strip and one side strip together, work 1 row of sc in every other matching st on edge of strips. (This will cause side strip to fold inward.) Work same joining with other side strip. With J crochet hook, work 1 row of color-over-color sc around entire joined piece, working 3 sc in each corner, join with sl st to first sc. Fasten off. Block firmly.

Handles: With K crochet hook and triple strands of burnt orange, crochet 6 chains 50 ch in length. Braid the

3 chains together to make an 18-inch handle. Make another braid for other handle in the same way.

Button Loop: With K crochet hook and double strands of burnt orange, make 3 chains 50 ch in length and braid together, as for handles. Sew the two ends of braid together to form a ring. Sew two sides of ring together at center to form a figure 8.

Positioning of Handles and Button Loop: Lay the piece flat with right side down, fold the right and left panels to the center of the blanket, fold the two short edges of the center panel inward to the center, and then fold the piece in half once again. Position the handles as shown in the black-and-white photograph and sew them in place. Sew the buttons in place as shown in the photo, one on each side of the folded blanket. Use the button loop to hold together the buttons.

Portable Plaid Lap Robe Chart

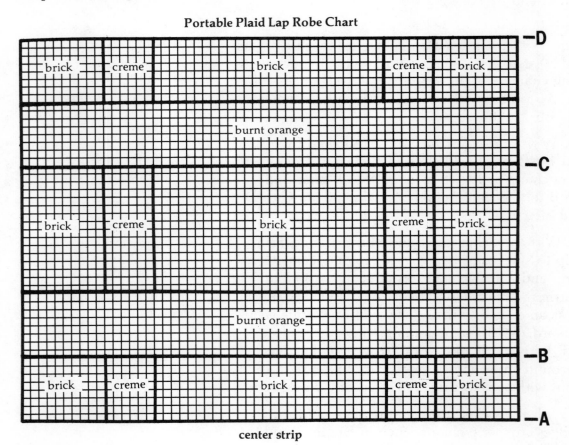

center strip

Portable Plaid Lap Robe Charts

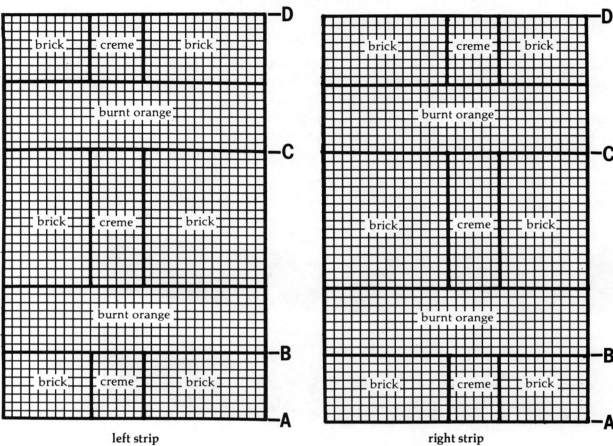

left strip

right strip

STRIPED SHAWL

Approximate finished size: 17 by 60 inches
No experience needed

Another perfect beginner's project, this knitted shawl in
bulky yarn goes everywhere. The only color changes are
in the easy stripe patterns at each end of the shawl. The
shawl can be lined with a soft material, which will add
to its comfort and help to stabilize the edges of the
stockinette-stitch knitting.

Materials:
Caron Rug and Craft Yarn, 1.6-ounce (70-yard) skeins
    5 skeins color 002, creme
    1 skein color 0013, brick
    1 skein color 0012, burnt orange
Knitting needles, No. 10½
Crochet hook, size J

Gauge: 3 stitches=1 inch; 4 rows=1 inch

Shawl: With creme, cast on 50 sts. *With creme, work even in stockinette st (k 1 row—right side; p 1 row—wrong side) for 8 rows. Continuing in stockinette st, work 8 rows brick, 8 rows creme, 8 rows burnt orange, 8 rows creme, 8 rows brick.* With creme, work even for 36 inches, end wrong side. Work stripe pattern between *'s in reverse. Bind off.

Finishing: With creme and crochet hook, work 1 row sc along each long edge, spacing sts so that work lies flat. Block piece firmly.

Fringe: Cut 8-inch lengths of yarn in creme. Knot 5 strands in every third st along each short edge of shawl.

STRIPED TRAVEL PILLOW

Approximate finished size: 17-inch square
Some experience needed

Add this travel pillow to your portable lap robe and
shawl and your traveling comfort will be complete.
Folded over, the pillow could fit into the lap-robe "bag."
When you work the vertical stripe on this design, be
sure to twist the new yarn with the old yarn to avoid
leaving gaps in the work.

Materials:
Caron Rug and Craft Yarn, 1.6-ounce (70-yard) skeins
    2 skeins color 002, creme
    1 skein color 0013, brick
    1 skein color 0012, burnt orange
Knitting needles, No. 10½
Crochet hook, size J
Two 19-inch squares of fabric
Sewing thread
Polyester stuffing

Gauge: 3 stitches=1 inch; 4 rows=1 inch

Knitted Pillow Cover: With creme, cast on 38 sts, followed by 6 sts burnt orange and 8 sts creme—52 sts. Work even in stockinette st (k 1 row—right side; p 1 row—wrong side) in colors as established for 8 rows. Change to brick and work even for 8 rows. Return to original colors of 8 sts creme, 6 sts burnt orange, and 38 sts creme and work even for 54 rows. Bind off.

Finishing: With creme, work 1 row sc around entire knitted piece, working 3 sc in each corner. Join with sl st to first st. Fasten off. Block lightly. Make a 17-inch-square pillow form from fabric, following general instructions at the beginning of the book. Sew knitted pillow cover to pillow form.

THE CROCHETED HOME

FRENCH PROVINCIAL
LIVING ROOM

FLOWERED LAP ROBE

Approximate finished size: 51 by 51 inches

No experience needed

This appliquéd lap robe could easily be expanded to afghan size by the addition of more squares. The flower-and-diamond design here was inspired by a lovely blue-and-white fabric used in the decorating of a French Provincial living room, although you can, of course, choose your own color scheme.

Materials:
Brunswick Windrush (100% Orlon Acrylic from Dupont), 100-gram (3.5-ounce) skeins
   7 skeins color 90721, denim heather
   3 skeins color 90400, Aran
   1 skein color 90112, medium powder blue

Crochet hook, size H
Sewing thread

Pattern Stitch for Squares: Make a chain of specified length.
Row 1: Ch 1, 1 sc in second ch from hook, 2 dc in same ch, *skip 2 ch, (1 sc, 2 dc) in next ch (shell made); repeat from * across, ending skip 2 ch, 1 sc in the last sc. Ch 1, turn.
Row 2: *Work 1 shell in next sc, skip 2 dc; repeat from * across, ending 1 sc in last sc. Ch 1, turn.
Repeat Row 2 for pat.

Gauge: 1 pattern stitch=1 inch for square pattern; each completed square measures 9 inches.

Squares: Make 25. With denim heather and size H hook, loosely ch 28. Work even in pat st for 19 rows. Do not turn. Work 1 row of sc around the square, working 20 sc along each side and 3 sc in each corner. Fasten off. With Aran, work 1 row of sc around each square in same manner, followed by 1 row of sc with medium powder blue. Fasten off.

Flowers: Make 25. With Aran, ch 4, join with sl st to form a ring. *Rnd 1:* *Ch 4, 2 tr in ring, ch 4, 1 sl st in ring; repeat from * 4 times more. Do not fasten off. Ch 8 for stem, (ch 6, turn, work 1 sc in second ch from hook, 1 hdc in next ch, 1 dc in next ch, 1 hdc in next ch, 1 sc in next ch, join with sl st to next ch on stem) twice to make two leaves, ch 4. Fasten off.

Finishing: Sew one flower in center of each square as shown in black-and-white photograph. Sew squares together as shown in placement diagram.

Border: *Rnd 1:* With Aran, join in any corner space and work 1 row of sc around entire joined piece, working 3 sc in each corner; join with sl st to first st. *Rnd 2:* Ch 1, *work 1 sc in next sc, ch 5, 1 sl st in third ch from hook, ch 2, skip 2 sc; repeat from * around joined piece, join with sl st to first sc. Fasten off.

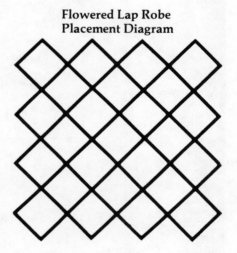

**Flowered Lap Robe
Placement Diagram**

FILET MESH PILLOW

Approximate finished size: 12 by 12 inches,
  not including border

No experience needed

The crocheted filet mesh on this little pillow creates an openwork pattern, which makes the selection of the fabric for the pillow form very important. In this case, we used a fabric matching the flowered lap robe, a blue shade light enough to show off the dark blue appliquéd flowers.

Materials:
Brunswick Windrush (100% Orlon Acrylic from Dupont), 100-gram (3.5-ounce) skeins
    1 skein color 90400, Aran
    1 skein color 90112, medium
      powder blue
Crochet hook, size H
Two 15-inch squares fabric, in light blue
Sewing thread
Polyester stuffing

Gauge: 3 squares (ch 2, 1 dc=1 square)=2 inches

Pillow: With Aran, ch 49.
Row 1 (wrong side): Starting in seventh ch from hook, *work 1 dc in next ch, ch 2, skip 2 ch; repeat from * across, end 1 dc in last ch—15 ch-2 sps. Ch 5, turn.
Row 2: Skip first dc, *1 dc in next dc, 2 dc in next ch-2 sp, 1 dc in next dc, ch 2; repeat from * across, ending 1 dc in third ch of turning ch-7. Ch 5, turn.
Row 3: Skip first dc, 1 dc in next dc, *ch 2, skip 2 dc, 1 dc in next dc, ch 2, 1 dc in next dc; repeat from * across, ending ch 2, 1 dc in third ch of turning ch-5. Ch 5, turn.
Row 4: Skip first dc, 1 dc in next dc, 2 dc in next ch-2 sp, 1 dc in next dc, *ch 2, 1 dc in next dc; repeat from * across to within last 2 squares of row, 2 dc in next-to-last ch-2 sp, 1 dc in next dc, ch 2, skip 2 ch, 1 dc in next ch. Ch 5, turn.
Note: On the following repeats of Row 3, follow the instructions to skip 2 dc only when they are side by side without ch-2 between them.
Repeat Rows 3 and 4 for 7 times more, followed by one repeat of Row 3. Work Row 2 once more, followed by one repeat of Row 3. Ch 1, turn. Do not fasten off.

Edging: *Rnd 1:* Work 1 row sc around edge of square, working 45 sc evenly spaced along each side and 3 sc in each corner, join with sl st to first sc.
Rnd 2: Ch 1, *work 1 sc in next sc, ch 5, 1 sl st in third ch from hook, ch 2, skip 2 sc; repeat from * around, join with sl st to first sc. Fasten off.

Flowers: Make 2. With medium powder blue, ch 4, join
92

with sl st to form a ring. *Rnd 1:* *Ch 4, 2 tr in ring, ch 4, 1 sl st in ring; repeat from * 4 times more. Do not fasten off. Ch 8 for stem, (ch 6, turn, work 1 sc in second ch from hook, 1 hdc in next ch, 1 dc in next ch, 1 hdc in next ch, 1 sc in next ch, join with sl st to next ch on stem) twice to make two leaves, ch 4. Fasten off.

Finishing: Make a 12-inch-square pillow form from light blue fabric, following general instructions at beginning of book. Sew crocheted piece to pillow, leaving Rnd 2 of edging free. Sew two flowers in place as shown in black-and-white photo.

LACY ROUND PILLOW

Approximate finished size: 15 inches in diameter
Some experience needed

This crocheted circle of dark blue lace stands out in
beautiful relief from the smooth fabric of the light blue
pillow. A white lace border could add another nice dimen-
sion to the pillow, if desired. The design looks more
complicated than it really is, so that a crocheter of
average experience should feel confident in attempting it.

Materials:

Brunswick Windrush (100% Orlon Acrylic from Dupont), 100-gram (3.5-ounce) skeins
1 skein color 90112, medium powder blue
Crochet hook, size H

Two 17-inch squares of fabric, in light blue
Sewing thread
Polyester stuffing

Gauge: 1 treble crochet=1 inch in height

Note: To work tr tog—work each tr to point where 1 loop remains on hook, leave loop on hook and complete specified number of tr in same manner, yo and draw through all loops on hook.

Pillow Cover: Ch 10, join with sl st to form a ring.

Rnd 1: Ch 4, work 2 tr tog in ring, *(ch 7, 3 tr tog in ring) 7 times, ch 7, join with sl st to fourth ch of starting ch-4.

Rnd 2: Work 1 sl st in next st, work (ch 4, 2 tr tog—counts as * 3-tr tog, ch 3, 1 tr, ch 3, 1 dc inserting hook in middle of post of tr just made, ch 3, 3 tr tog) all in same ch-7 sp; repeat from * in each ch-7 sp around, join with sl st to fourth ch of starting ch-4.

Rnd 3: Ch 8, skip first ch-3 sp, *(3 tr tog, ch 3, 1 tr, ch 3, 1 dc inserting hook in middle of post of tr just made, ch 3, 3 tr tog) all in next ch-3 sp between tr and dc, ch 4, 1 tr between next 2 tr groups, ch 4; repeat from * around, (3 tr tog, ch 3, 1 tr, ch 3, 1 dc inserting hook in middle of post of tr just made, ch 3, 3 tr tog) all in next ch-3 sp between tr and dc, ch 4, join with sl st to fourth ch of starting ch-8.

Rnd 4: Ch 8, skip first ch-3 sp, *(3 tr tog, ch 3, 1 tr, ch 3, 1 dc inserting hook in middle of post of tr just made, ch 3, 3 tr tog) all in next ch-3 sp between tr and dc, ch 4, 1 tr in next tr, ch 4; repeat from * around, (3 tr tog, ch 3, 1 tr, ch 3, 1 dc inserting hook in middle of post of tr just made, ch 3, 3 tr tog) all in next ch-3 sp between tr and dc, ch 4, join with sl st to fourth ch of starting ch-8.

Rnd 5: Ch 10, work as for Rnd 4, except ch 6 before and after solitary tr sts, end by joining with 1 sl st in fourth ch of starting ch-10.

Rnd 6: Ch 11, work as for Rnd 5, except ch 7 before

and after solitary tr sts, end by joining with 1 sl st in fourth ch of starting ch-11. Fasten off.

Finishing: Make a 15-inch-round pillow form from light blue fabric, following general instructions at beginning of book. Sew crocheted piece to pillow.

RUFFLED DOILY

Approximate finished size: 14½ inches in diameter
No experience needed

This simple chain-mesh doily with ruffled edge makes a
beautiful frame for an antique lamp or a painted vase
full of fresh flowers. Like the Lacy Round Pillow, it
looks more complicated than it really is. The edge
ruffles naturally, and since the yarn used is knitting-
worsted weight, no starching is necessary to maintain it.

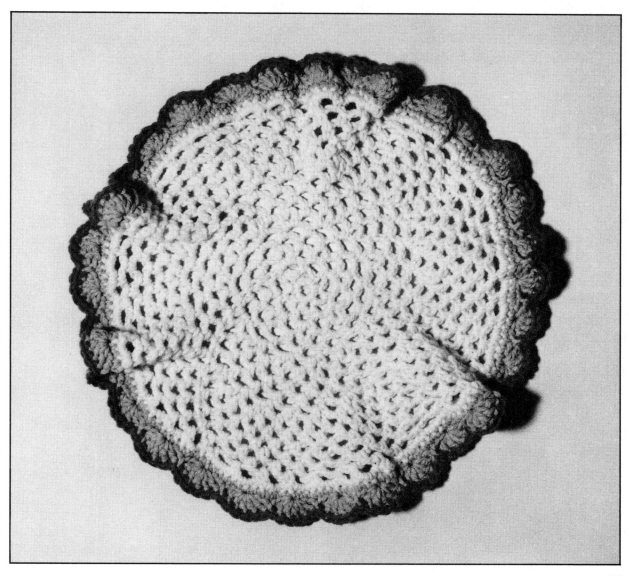

Materials:
Brunswick Windrush (100% Orlon Acrylic from Dupont),
100-gram (3.5-ounce) skeins
  1 skein color 90400, Aran
  1 skein color 90721, denim heather
  1 skein color 90112, medium powder blue
Crochet hook, size H

Gauge: 5-round circle = 4½ inches

Doily: Ch 4, join with sl st to form a ring.
Rnd 1: Ch 1, (1 sc in ring, ch 3) 7 times, join with sl st to first sc.
Rnd 2: Work 1 sl st in next ch, 1 sc in same ch-3 sp, *(ch 3, 1 sc in next ch-3 sp) 6 times, ch 3, join with sl st to first sc.
Rnd 3: Work 1 sl st in next ch, 1 sc in same ch-3 sp, ch 3, 1 sc in same ch-3 sp, *ch 3, 1 sc in next ch-3 sp, ch 3, 1 sc in same ch-3 sp; repeat from * around ch 3, join with sl st to first sc.
Rnd 4: Work 1 sl st in next ch, 1 sc in same ch-3 sp, *ch 3, 1 sc in next ch-3 sp; repeat from * around, end ch 3, join with sl st to first sc.
Repeat Rnd 4 once more. Work Rnd 3 once more, followed by 3 repeats of Rnd 4. Work Rnd 3, followed by 5 repeats of Rnd 4.

Ending: *Rnd 1:* With Aran, work 1 sc in each sc and 3 sc in each ch-3 sp around. Fasten off. *Rnd 2:* With denim heather, work 1 sc in each sc around, join with sl st to first st. *Rnd 3:* Ch 2, work 4 dc in same sc, *skip 2 sc, 1 sl st in next sc, skip 2 sc, 5 dc in next sc; repeat from * around, end skip 2 sc, join with sl st to first st. Fasten off. *Rnd 4:* With medium powder blue, work 1 sc in each sc and 1 sl st in each sl st around, join with sl st to first st. Fasten off.

DECO MASTER BEDROOM

RIPPLE AFGHAN

Approximate finished size: 45 by 50 inches

No experience needed

The traditional ripple afghan is worked here in high-contrast Art Deco colors. This pattern is one of the most popular of all crocheted designs and no afghan collection could be considered complete without one. This dramatic tassled throw would be particularly striking draped over a satin bedspread.

Materials:
Brunswick Windrush (100% Orlon Acrylic from Dupont), 100-gram (3.5-ounce) skeins
    6 skeins color 9060, black
    1 skein color 90621, grey heather
    1 skein color 9015, pink heather
Crochet hook, size H

Pattern Stitch: Make a chain of specified length.
Row 1: Ch 2, work 1 dc in third ch from hook, 1 dc in each of next 8 ch, *3 dc in next ch, 1 dc in each of next 9 ch, skip 2 ch, 1 dc in each of next 9 ch, repeat from * across, end 2 dc in last ch. Turn.
Row 2: Working through back loops only, ch 2, skip first dc, *1 dc in each of next 9 dc, skip 2 dc, 1 dc in each of next 9 dc, 3 dc in next dc, repeat from * across to within last 10 dc, end 1 dc in each of next 8 dc, skip 1 dc, 1 dc through both loops of last dc. Turn.
Row 3: Working through back loops only, ch 2, skip first dc, *1 dc in each of next 9 dc, 3 dc in next dc, 1 dc in each of next 9 dc, skip 2 dc, repeat from * across, end 1 dc in each of next 8 dc, 3 dc in second ch of turning ch-2. Turn.
Repeat Rows 2 and 3 for pat.

Gauge: 7 double crochet=2 inches; 10 rows=7 inches in pattern stitch

Afghan: With black, ch 178. Then working in pat st throughout, work in color pat of *8 rows black, 2 rows grey heather, 8 rows black, 2 rows pink heather, repeat from * twice more, end 8 rows black, 2 rows grey heather, 8 rows black. Fasten off.

Tassels: Make 18. For each tassel, with black, cut twenty-three 15-inch strands and tie a 5-inch strand around the middle. Fold the strands in half at the tie, wrap one end of one of the strands securely around the folded strands 1 inch below the tie, fasten off, and trim the ends evenly. Tie one tassel at each point along both short edges of afghan.

TEXTURED PILLOW

Approximate finished size: 16 by 16 inches
Some experience needed

These highly textured pillow fronts pick up the
highlighted colors of pink and grey on the Ripple
Afghan and are backed with pillow forms made from
black satin. The filet mesh in the corners of each pillow
gives an appearance of cutwork where the black satin
shows through.

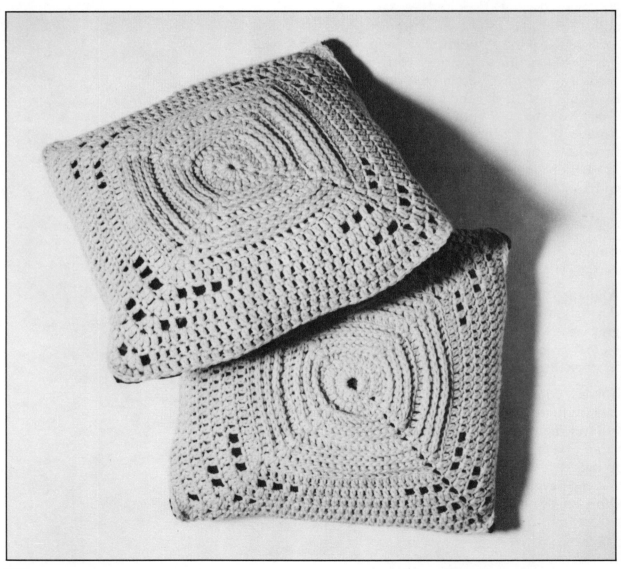

Materials:
Brunswick Windrush (100% Orlon Acrylic from Dupont),
100-gram (3.5-ounce) skeins
    1 skein color 9015, pink heather
Crochet hook, size H
Two 18-inch satin squares in black
Sewing thread
Polyester stuffing

Gauge: 11 double crochet=4 inches

Pillow Cover: Ch 8, join with sl st to form a ring.
Rnd 1: Ch 2 (counts as 1 dc), work 15 dc in ring, join
with sl st to second ch of starting ch-2.
Rnd 2: Ch 2 (counts as 1 dc), *work 2 dc in next dc,
1 dc in next dc, repeat from * around, end 2 dc in next
dc—24 dc, join with sl st to second ch of starting ch-2.
Rnd 3: Ch 2 (counts as 1 dc), work 1 dc in each of next
4 dc, *3 dc in next dc, 1 dc in each of next 5 dc, repeat
from * 2 times more, end 3 dc in last dc— 32 dc, join
with sl st to second ch of starting ch-2.
Rnds 4, 5 and 6: Ch 1 at beg of each rnd, work 3 dc in
center dc of each 3-dc corner group, and, around each
dc along side of square, work 1 back post dc—insert
hook from back to front to back around post of dc
below and complete 1 dc, join with sl st to second ch of
starting ch-2.
Rnd 7: Work 3 dc through both loops in center dc of
each 3-dc corner group and 1 dc through back loops
only in each dc along each side of square.
Rnds 8, 9, and 10: Work as for Rnds 4, 5, and 6.
Rnd 11: Work as for Rnd 7.
Rnd 12: Working through both loops now, work 1 dc in
each dc and 3 dc in center dc of each corner, working
[(ch 1, skip 1 dc, 1 dc in next dc) 2 times, ch 1, skip
1 dc] before and after each 3-dc corner.
Rnd 13: Work as for Rnd 11, but work through
both loops.
Rnd 14: Working through both loops, work 1 dc in each
dc and 3 dc in center dc of each corner, working (ch 1,
skip 1 dc in next dc, ch 1) before and after each
3-dc corner.
Rnd 15: Work as for Rnd 13.

Rnd 16: Working through both loops now, work 1 dc in each dc and 3 dc in center dc of each corner, working (ch 1, skip 1 dc) before and after each 3-dc corner.
Rnd 17: Work as for Rnd 15. Fasten off.

Finishing: Make a 16-inch-square pillow form from black satin fabric, following general instructions at beginning of book. Sew crocheted piece to pillow.

FILET MESH RUG

Approximate finished size: 42 by 46 inches
Some experience needed

Our rug is made with double strands of yarn and gives the appearance of cutwork when the flooring shows through. It is actually quite quick and easy to crochet once the pattern has been clearly established, and it is a striking complement to the other projects in our Art Deco bedroom.

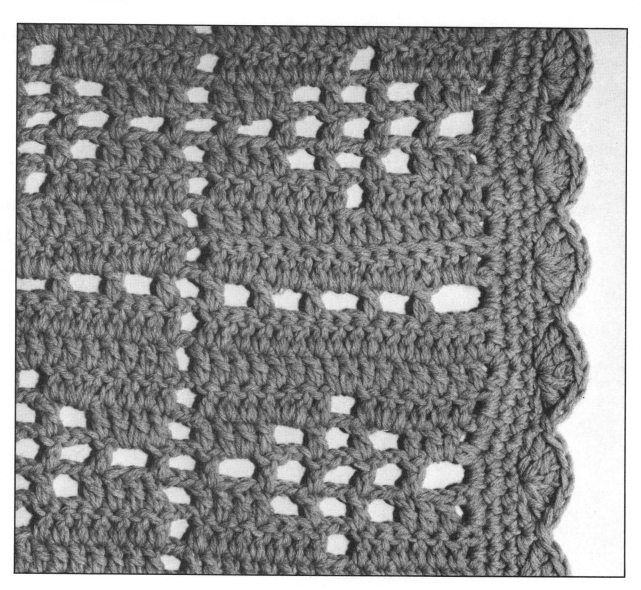

Materials:
Brunswick Windrush (100% Orlon Acrylic from Dupont),
100-gram (3.5-ounce) skeins
    8 skeins color 90621, grey heather
Crochet hook, size K

Note: Crochet with double strands of yarn throughout.
Ch 2 (counts as 1 dc) at beg of each row. Skip first dc
of each row. Work last dc of row into second ch of ch-2
of previous row.

Gauge: 8 double crochet=3 inches

Rug: With double strands of yarn, ch 109.
Row 1: Work 1 dc in seventh ch from hook, *ch 2, skip
2, 1 dc in next ch; repeat from * across—first row of
chart completed.
Row 2: Now follow chart, repeating from A to B 5
times across, end by working chart from A to C once.
Continue to work chart to completion, repeating rows
from A to D 4 times and from A to E once. Fasten off.

Border: Work 3 rnds sc around entire piece, working
3 sc in each corner. *Scallop Edging:* Join yarn in any
corner st, *skip 2 sc, work 5 dc in next sc, skip 2 sc,
1 sc in next sc; repeat from * around. Join with sl st to
first sc. Fasten off.

Filet Mesh Rug Chart

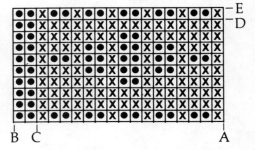

Stitch Key
X=1 dc
•• =ch-2 space

PREPPY PLAIDS
FOR A BOY'S ROOM

BLUE PLAID LAP ROBE

Approximate finished size: 43 by 51 inches
Experience needed

The texture and weaving patterns of this blue plaid lap
robe are clearly shown in the accompanying photograph.
The crochet work involved takes a little concentration,
but the striking plaid you create with woven chains
of yellow and dark blue is well worth the effort.

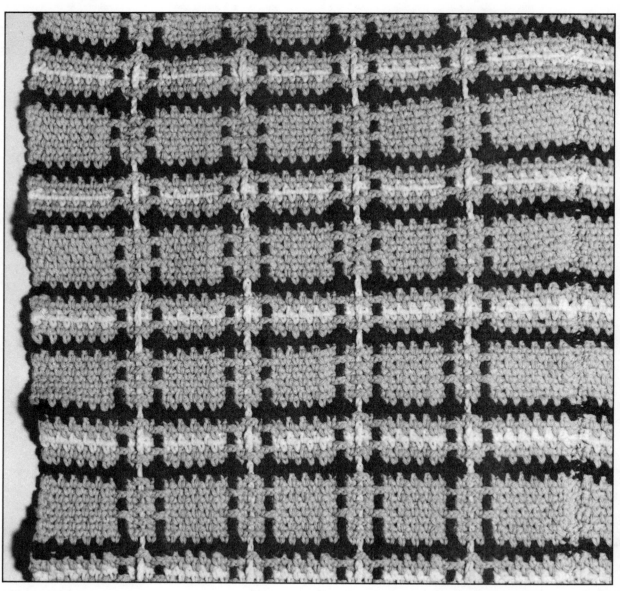

Materials:
Lion Brand Sayelle, 100-gram (3.5-ounce) skeins
    8 skeins color 109, colonial blue
    3 skeins color 107, robin blue
    1 skein color 197, radiant yellow
Crochet hook, size H

Gauge: 9 stitches=2 inches; 9 rows=2 inches

Strips: Makes 3. With colonial blue, ch 78.
Row 1: Starting in second ch from hook, *(work 1 sc in next ch, ch 1, skip 1 ch) 4 times, work 1 sc in next ch, (ch 2, skip 2 ch, 1 sc in next ch) 2 times, ch 2, skip 2 ch; repeat from * 3 times more, end (1 sc in next ch, ch 1, skip 1 ch) 4 times, 1 sc in last ch. Ch 1, turn.
Row 2: Work 1 sc in first sc, *(1 sc in next ch-1 sp, ch 1, skip next sc) 3 times, 1 sc in next ch-1 sp, 1 sc in next sc, (ch 2, skip 2 ch, 1 sc in next sc) 2 times, ch 2, skip 2 ch, 1 sc in next sc; repeat from * 3 times more, end (1 sc in next ch-1 sp, ch 1, skip next sc) 2 times, 1 sc in last ch-1 sp, 1 sc in last sc.
Ch 1, turn.
Row 3: *Work 1 sc in first sc, (ch 1, skip 1 sc, 1 sc in next ch-1 sp) 3 times, ch 1, skip 1 sc, 1 sc in next sc, *(ch 2, skip 2 ch, 1 sc in next sc) 2 times, ch 2, 1 sc in next sc, (ch 1, 1 sc in next ch-1 sp) 3 times, ch 1, 1 sc in last sc; repeat from * across.
Repeat Rows 2 and 3 for pat st, *at same time,* work in color pat of * 8 rows colonial blue, 2 rows robin blue, 2 rows colonial blue, 2 rows radiant yellow, 2 rows colonial blue, 2 rows robin blue; repeat from * 11 times more, end with 8 rows colonial blue.

Finishing: Sew strips together, matching stripes. Crochet 12 radiant yellow and 24 robin blue chains long enough to weave through vertical length of afghan. Weave crocheted chains through ch-2 spaces as shown in black-and-white photograph. Be sure to weave robin blue chains under robin blue crocheted stripes and radiant yellow chains under radiant yellow crocheted stripes. With robin blue, work 1 row of sc along each short edge of finished piece.

BLUE PLAID PILLOW

Approximate finished size: 14 by 15½ inches
Experience needed

The crocheted plaid used in this pillow is the same one used in the Blue Plaid Lap Robe. We've crocheted both sides of this pillow, but you could crochet one side only. You might also try a reverse plaid, using the dark blue as the main color and the lighter blue and yellow for the chains.

Materials:

Lion Brand Sayelle, 100-gram (3.5-ounce) skeins
  2 skeins color 109, colonial blue
  1 skein color 107, robin blue
  1 skein color 197, radiant yellow

Crochet hook, size H
Two 18-inch squares of fabric, in light blue
Sewing thread
Polyester stuffing

Gauge: 9 stitches=2 inches; 9 rows=2 inches

Pillow Cover: Make 2. With colonial blue, ch 78.

Row 1: Starting in second ch from hook, *(work 1 sc in next ch, ch 1, skip 1 ch) 4 times, work 1 sc in next ch, (ch 2, skip 2 ch, 1 sc in next ch) 2 times, ch 2, skip 2 ch; repeat from * 3 times more, end (1 sc in next ch, ch 1, skip 1 ch) 4 times, 1 sc in last ch. Ch 1, turn.

Row 2: Work 1 sc in first sc, *(1 sc in next ch-1 sp, ch 1, skip next sc) 3 times, 1 sc in next ch-1 sp, 1 sc in next sc, (ch 2, skip 2 ch, 1 sc in next sc) 2 times, ch 2, skip 2 ch, 1 sc in next sc; repeat from * 3 times more, end (1 sc in next ch-1 sp, ch 1, skip next sc) 2 times, 1 sc in last ch-1 sp, 1 sc in last sc. Ch 1, turn.

Row 3: Work 1 sc in first sc, (ch 1, skip 1 sc, 1 sc in next ch-1 sp) 3 times, ch 1, skip 1 sc, 1 sc in next sc, *(ch 2, skip 2 ch, 1 sc in next sc) 2 times, ch 2, 1 sc in next sc, (ch 1, 1 sc in next ch-1 sp) 3 times, ch 1, 1 sc in last sc; repeat from * across.

Repeat Rows 2 and 3 for pat st, *at same time*, work in color pat of *8 rows colonial blue, 2 rows robin blue, 2 rows colonial blue, 2 rows radiant yellow, 2 rows colonial blue, 2 rows robin blue; repeat from * 2 times more, end with 8 rows colonial blue.

Finishing: Crochet 4 radiant yellow and 8 robin blue chains long enough to weave through vertical length of each finished piece. Weave crocheted chains through ch-2 spaces as shown in black-and-white photograph. Be sure to weave robin blue chains under robin blue crocheted stripes and radiant yellow chains under radiant yellow crocheted stripes. Make a 15½-inch-wide by 14-inch-high pillow form from light blue fabric, following general instructions at beginning of book. Sew pillow cover to pillow form.

HASSOCK COVER

Approximate finished size: General instructions for any size hassock are given

Experience needed

The instructions for creating a strip of plaid of the general size needed for covering a hassock are included. You can make your own hassock with a long strip of heavy-duty canvas to form the sides and two circles for the top and bottom. Join the sides and bottom, line with cotton batting, and stuff with crumpled newspaper. Then line the top with more cotton batting and sew the top fabric piece in place.

Materials:

Lion Brand Sayelle, 100-gram
(3.5-ounce) skeins
    about 3 skeins color 109, colonial
      blue, depending on length of strip
    1 skein color 107, robin blue
    1 skein color 197, radiant yellow

Crochet hook, size H
Optional: Fabric, in light blue, to cover
    top and bottom of your hassock.

Gauge: 9 stitches=2 inches; 9 rows=2 inches

Hassock Cover: With colonial blue, ch 61. (*Note:* This
will make a 13-inch-wide strip—you may adjust the
width to match the height of your own hassock.)

Row 1: Starting in second ch from hook, *(work 1 sc in
next ch, ch 1, skip 1 ch) 4 times, work 1 sc in next ch,
(ch 2, skip 2 ch, 1 sc in next ch) 2 times, ch 2, skip 2 ch;
repeat from * 2 times more, end (1 sc in next ch, ch 1,
skip 1 ch) 4 times, 1 sc in last ch. Ch 1, turn.

Row 2: Work 1 sc in first sc, *(1 sc in next ch-1 sp,
ch 1, skip next sc) 3 times, 1 sc in next ch-1 sp, 1 sc in
next sc, (ch 2, skip 2 ch, 1 sc in next sc) 2 times, ch 2,
skip 2 ch, 1 sc in next sc; repeat from * 2 times more,
end (1 sc in next ch-1 sp, ch 1, skip next sc) 2 times,
1 sc in last ch-1 sp, 1 sc in last sc. Ch 1, turn.

Row 3: Work 1 sc in first sc, (ch 1, skip 1 sc, 1 sc in
next ch-1 sp) 3 times, ch 1, skip 1 sc, 1 sc in next sc,
*(ch 2, skip 2 ch, 1 sc in next sc) 2 times, ch 2, 1 sc in
next sc, (ch 1, 1 sc in next ch-1 sp) 3 times, ch 1, 1 sc in
last sc; repeat from * 3 times.

Repeat Rows 2 and 3 for pat st, *at same time*, work in
color pat of *8 rows colonial blue, 2 rows robin blue, 2
rows colonial blue, 2 rows radiant yellow, 2 rows
colonial blue, 2 rows robin blue; repeat from * until
piece measures long enough to reach around your
hassock (ours measured 45 inches). Fasten off.

Finishing: Crochet chains of radiant yellow and robin
blue long enough to weave through length of strip.
Weave crocheted chains through ch-2 spaces as shown
in black-and-white photograph. Be sure to weave robin
blue chains under robin blue crocheted stripes and radiant yellow chains under radiant yellow crocheted stripes.
Sew hassock cover around sides of hassock. If desired,
cover top of hassock in matching fabric, as we did.

113

VICTORIAN GIRL'S ROOM

VICTORIAN AFGHAN

Approximate finished size: 45 by 54 inches
Some experience needed

Lavender and white and very lovely, indeed, is this
fantasy afghan for a young girl's room. The squares are
joined as you go, so that when you finish, no sewing is
necessary. The squares themselves are easy to make and
only a little experience is necessary to join the squares as
you crochet.

Materials:
Brunswick Windrush (100% Orlon Acrylic from Dupont),
100-gram (3.5-ounce) skeins
    5 skeins color 9010, white
    3 skeins color 90025, sugar plum
Crochet hook, size H

Gauge: Each square=8½ inches

Basic Square: With sugar plum, ch 6, join with sl st to form a ring.

Rnd 1: Ch 1, *3 sc in ring, (ch 3, 1 sl st in third ch from hook—picot made); repeat from * 3 times more, join with sl st to first st. Fasten off.

Rnd 2: Join white in any center sc of 3-sc group, ch 8, *1 dc in center sc of next 3-sc group, ch 6; repeat from * 2 times more, join with sl st to second ch of starting ch-3.

Rnd 3: Ch 3, *ch 3, (5 dc, ch 3, 5 dc) in next ch-6 loop; repeat from * 3 times more, end last repeat with 4 dc, join with sl st to third ch of starting ch-3.

Rnd 4: Ch 3; 2 dc, ch 3, 3 dc in same sp—first corner, *ch 3, (1 sc, ch 3, 1 sc) in next ch-3 sp, ch 3, (3 dc, ch 3, 3 dc) in next ch-3 sp; repeat from * twice more, end ch 3, (1 sc, ch 3, 1 sc) in next ch-3 sp, ch 3, join with sl st to third ch of starting ch-3.

Rnd 5: Work 1 sl st in each of next 2 dc, 1 sl st in next ch-3 sp, ch 3, (2 dc, ch 3, 3 dc) in next corner sp, *ch 2, picot, ch 2, (1 sc, ch 3, 1 sc) in next ch-3 between 2 sc, ch 2, picot, ch 2, (3 dc, ch 3, 3 dc) in next corner; repeat from * 2 times more, end ch 2, picot, ch 2, (1 sc, ch 3, 1 sc) in next ch-3 between 2 sc, ch 2, picot, ch 2, join with sl st in third ch of starting ch-3.

Rnd 6: Work 1 sl st in each of next 2 dc and ch-3 sp, ch 3, (2 dc, ch 3, 3 dc) in same ch-3 sp, *ch 1, 3 dc in third dc of next 3-dc group, ch 1, 4 dc in next ch-3 sp, ch 1, 3 dc in next dc, ch 1, (3 dc, ch 3, 3 dc) in next corner sp; repeat from * 2 times more, end ch 1, 3 dc in third dc of next 3-dc group, ch 1, 4 dc in next ch-3 sp, ch 1, 3 dc in next dc, ch 1, join with sl st to starting ch-3. Fasten off.

Rnd 7: With sugar plum, join in any ch-3 corner sp, ch 3, (2 dc, ch 1, picot, ch 1, 3 dc) in same ch-3 sp,

117

*(ch 1, picot, ch 1, 3 dc in next ch-1 sp) twice, ch 1, picot, ch 1, skip 4 dc, 3 dc in next ch-1 sp, ch 1, picot, ch 1, 3 dc in next ch-1 sp, ch 1, picot, ch 1, (3 dc, ch 1, picot, ch 1, 3 dc) in next corner sp; repeat from * 2 times more, (ch 1, picot, ch 1, 3 dc in next ch-1 sp) twice, ch 1, picot, ch 1, skip 4 dc, 3 dc in next ch-1 sp, ch 1, picot, ch 1, 3 dc in next ch-1 sp, ch 1, picot, ch 1, join with sl st to third ch of starting ch-3.

To Join Additional Squares: Work as for Basic Square, and join additional squares on Rnd 7 in picots as follows: Ch 3, remove hook and insert in matching picot of adjacent square, pull dropped loop through picot, ch 1, 1 sl st in second ch of starting ch-3, ch 1, continue to work 3-dc groups between picots as established on Basic Square of Rnd. 7. Join on as many sides as necessary, joining in each picot, including corner picot. Work 28 additional squares in this manner, for a total of 30 squares, joined on Rnd 7 in five- by six-square arrangement.

Border: *Rnd 1:* With sugar plum, join in any picot, work 1 sc in same picot, *ch 7, 1 sc in next picot; repeat from * around, join with sl st to first sc. *Rnd 2:* Ch 1, work 7 sc in each ch-7 1p and 1 sl st in each sc, join with sl st to first sc. *Rnd 3:* *Skip first of 7-sc, 1 hdc in second and third sc, ch 4, work 1 sl st in third ch from hook, ch 1, skip fourth sc, 1 hdc in fifth and sixth sc, ch 1, skip seventh sc; repeat from * around. Fasten off.

VICTORIAN ROLL PILLOW

Approximate finished size: 27 inches long by 27 inches in
*   circumference*

Some experience needed

A lovely accent piece to accompany the Victorian Afghan, this roll pillow, made with the same granny-type squares, would look lovely on an antique, white-painted metal or brass bed. Other Victorian accents, such as needlepoint pictures, satin sachet pillows, oil lamps, and fancy mirror frames, would be charming in such a room.

Materials:
Brunswick Windrush (100% Orlon Acrylic from Dupont),
100-gram (3.5-ounce) skeins
    2 skeins color 9010, white
    1 skein color 90025, sugar plum
Crochet hook, size H
One 29-inch piece of fabric, in lavender
Two 9½-inch circles of fabric, in lavender
Sewing thread
Polyester stuffing

Gauge: Each square = 8½ inches

Basic Square: With sugar plum, ch 6, join with sl st to
form a ring.
Rnd 1: Ch 1, *3 sc in ring, (ch 3, 1 sl st in third ch from
hook—picot made); repeat from * 3 times more, join
with sl st to first st. Fasten off.
Rnd 2: Join white in any center sc of 3-sc group, ch 8,
*1 dc in center sc of next 3-sc group, ch 6; repeat from *
2 times more, join with sl st to second ch of starting ch-3.
Rnd 3: Ch 3, *ch 3, (5 dc, ch 3, 5 dc) in next ch-6 loop;
repeat from * 3 times more, end last repeat with 4 dc,
join with sl st to third ch of starting ch-3.
Rnd 4: Ch 3, 2 dc, ch 3, 3 dc in same sp—first corner,
*ch 3, (1 sc, ch 3, 1 sc) in next ch-3 sp, ch 3, (3 dc,
ch 3, 3 dc) in next ch-3 sp; repeat from * twice more,
end ch 3, (1 sc, ch 3, 1 sc) in next ch-3 sp, ch 3, join
with sl st to third ch of starting ch-3.
Rnd 5: Work 1 sl st in each of next 2 dc, 1 sl st in next
ch-3 sp, ch 3, (2 dc, ch 3, 3 dc) in next corner sp, *ch 2,
picot, ch 2, (1 sc, ch 3, 1 sc) in next ch-3 between 2 sc,
ch 2, picot, ch 2, (3 dc, ch 3, 3 dc) in next corner;
repeat from * 2 times more, end ch 2, picot, ch 2, (1 sc,
ch 3, 1 sc) in next ch-3 between 2 sc, ch 2, picot, ch 2,
join with sl st in third ch of starting ch-3.
Rnd 6: Work 1 sl st in each of next 2 dc and ch-3 sp, ch 3,
(2 dc, ch 3, 3 dc) in same ch-3 sp, *ch 1, 3 dc in third
dc of next 3-dc group, ch 1, 4 dc in next ch-3 sp, ch 1,
3 dc in next dc, ch 1, (3 dc, ch 3, 3 dc) in next corner
sp; repeat from * 2 times more, end ch 1, 3 dc in third
dc of next 3-dc group, ch 1, 4 dc in next ch-3 sp, ch 1,
3 dc in next dc, ch 1, join with sl st to starting ch-3.
Fasten off.

Rnd 7: With sugar plum, join in any ch-3 corner sp, ch 3, (2 dc, ch 1, picot, ch 1, 3 dc) in same ch-3 sp, *(ch 1, picot, ch 1, 3 dc in next ch-1 sp) twice, ch 1, picot, ch 1, skip 4 dc, 3 dc in next ch-1 sp, ch 1, picot, ch 1, 3 dc in next ch-1 sp, ch 1, picot, ch 1, (3 dc, ch 1, picot, ch 1, 3 dc) in next corner sp; repeat from * 2 times more, (ch 1, picot, ch 1, 3 dc in next ch-1 sp) twice, ch 1, picot, ch 1, skip 4 dc, 3 dc in next ch-1 sp, ch 1, picot, ch 1, 3 dc in next ch-1 sp, ch 1, picot, ch 1, join with sl st to third ch of starting ch-3.

To Join Additional Squares: Work as for Basic Square, and join additional squares on Rnd 7 in picots as follows: Ch 3, remove hook and insert in matching picot of adjacent square, pull dropped loop through picot, ch 1, 1 sl st in second ch of starting ch-3, ch 1, continue to work 3-dc groups between picots as established on Basic Square of Rnd 7. Join on as many sides as necessary, joining in each picot, including corner picot. Work 7 additional squares in this manner, for a total of 9 squares, joined on Rnd 7 in a three- by three-square arrangement.

Finishing: With right sides of fabric together, fold fabric in half and sew together along one 29-inch side of fabric, making a 1-inch seam. Trim seam allowance. With sewing thread, lightly gather circle ½ inch in from outer edge. Pulling thread slightly, gather to fit into open end of joined piece. Baste in place. Repeat with remaining circle on other end of piece, leaving an opening. Turn right side out and stuff pillow firmly. Sew opening. Place crocheted piece around pillow form and sew one end to the other at the picots. Sew edge of crocheted piece firmly in place around each round end of pillow along seamline.

VICTORIAN CHAIR CUSHION

*Approximate finished size: 13 inches square, not
    including ruffle*
Some experience needed

The deeply ruffled border on this lacy chair cushion is
charming on an antique rocker or the stool for a vanity
table. Fabric in a light lavender was used to make the
form for the cushion and it shows through the granny
squares on top. The cushion can be made to any size by
working more or fewer granny squares.

Materials:
Brunswick Windrush (100% Orlon Acrylic from Dupont),
100-gram (3.5-ounce) skeins
    1 skein color 9010, white
    1 skein color 90025, sugar plum
Crochet hook, size H
Two 15-inch squares of fabric, in lavender
Cotton batting or polyester stuffing
Sewing thread

Gauge: Each square＝6½ inches

Basic Square: With sugar plum, ch 6, join with sl st to
form a ring.
Rnd 1: Ch 1, *3 sc in ring, (ch 3, 1 sl st in third ch from
hook—picot made); repeat from * 3 times more, join
with sl st to first st. Fasten off.
Rnd 2: Join white in any center sc of 3-sc group, ch 8,
*1 dc in center sc of next 3-sc group, ch 6; repeat from
* 2 times more, join with sl st to second ch of starting ch-3.
Rnd 3: Ch 3, *ch 3, (5 dc, ch 3, 5 dc) in next ch-6 loop;
repeat from * 3 times more, end last repeat with 4 dc,
join with sl st to third ch of starting ch-3.
Rnd 4: Ch 3, 2 dc, ch 3, 3 dc in same sp—first corner,
*ch 3, (1 sc, ch 3, 1 sc) in next ch-3 sp, ch 3, (3 dc,
ch 3, 3 dc) in next ch-3 sp; repeat from * twice more,
end ch 3, (1 sc, ch 3, 1 sc) in next ch-3 sp, ch 3, join
with sl st to third ch of starting ch-3. Fasten off.
Rnd 5: With sugar plum, join in any ch-3 corner sp,
ch 3, (2 dc, ch 1, picot, ch 1, 3 dc) in same ch-3 sp,
*(ch 1, picot, ch 1, 3 dc in next ch-3 sp) twice, ch 1,
picot, ch 1, (3 dc, ch 1, picot, ch 1, 3 dc) in same ch-3
sp; repeat from * 2 times more, end (ch 1, picot, ch 1,
3 dc in next ch-3 sp) twice, ch 1, picot, ch 1, join with sl
st to third ch of starting ch-3. Fasten off.

To Join Additional Squares: Work as for Basic Square,
and join additional squares on Rnd 5 in picots as
follows: Ch 3, remove hook and insert in matching
picot of adjacent square, pull dropped loop through
picot, ch 1, 1 sl st in second ch of starting ch-3, ch 1,
continue to work 3-dc groups between picots as
established on Rnd 7. Join on as many sides as

necessary, joining in each picot, including corner picot. Work 2 additional squares in this manner, for a total of four squares joined on Rnd 7 in a two- by two-square arrangement.

Edging: *Rnd 1:* Join sugar plum in any picot, work 1 sc in same picot, *ch 3, 1 sc in center dc of next 3-dc group, ch 3, 1 sc in next picot; repeat from * around, join with sl st to first sc. *Rnd 2:* Work 3 dc in each ch-3 sp, 3 dc in each sc in picot, and 1 dc in each sc in center dc of next 3-dc group, join with sl st to first st. *Rnd 3:* Work 1 dc in each dc around, join with sl st to first st.

Finishing: Make one 13-inch-square pillow form from lavender fabric, following general instructions at beginning of book, stuffing with polyester stuffing or cotton batting cut to size. Sew crocheted piece to pillow, leaving ruffled edge free.

VICTORIAN NIGHT TABLE SKIRT

Approximate finished size: Skirt can be made to fit your table
Some experience needed

This project is made chiefly of fabric but with the accent
of the same granny squares used in making the afghan
and roll pillow in this set for a Victorian girl's room.
Instructions for custom-making a skirt for your
particular night table are included.

Materials:

Brunswick Windrush (100% Orlon Acrylic from Dupont), 100-gram (3.5-ounce) skeins

    1 skein color 9010, white, for every 8 squares

    1 skein color 90025, sugar plum, for every

        14 squares

Crochet hook, size H

Fabric, in lavender (see "Finishing" instructions

    following for measurements)

Sewing thread

Gauge: Each square＝8½ inches

Note: Measure the distance around your night table and calculate the number of squares needed to fit around, overlapping them at the back if necessary.

Basic Square: With sugar plum, ch 6, join with sl st to form a ring.

Rnd 1: Ch 1, *3 sc in ring, (ch 3, 1 sl st in third ch from hook—picot made); repeat from * 3 times more, join with sl st to first st. Fasten off.

Rnd 2: Join white in any center sc of 3-sc group, ch 8, *1 dc in center sc of next 3-sc group, ch 6; repeat from * 2 times more, join with sl st to second ch of starting ch-3.

Rnd 3: Ch 3, *ch 3, (5 dc, ch 3, 5 dc) in next ch-6 loop; repeat from * 3 times more, end last repeat with 4 dc, join with sl st to third ch of starting ch-3.

Rnd 4. Ch 3, 2 dc, ch 3, 3 dc in same sp—first corner, *ch 3, (1 sc, ch 3, 1 sc) in next ch-3 sp, ch 3, (3 dc, ch 3, 3 dc) in next ch-3 sp; repeat from * twice more, end ch 3, (1 sc, ch 3, 1 sc) in next ch-3 sp, ch 3, join with sl st to third ch of starting ch-3.

Rnd 5: Work 1 sl st in each of next 2 dc, 1 sl st in next ch-3 sp, ch 3, (2 dc, ch 3, 3 dc) in next corner sp, *ch 2, picot, ch 2, (1 sc, ch 3, 1 sc) in next ch-3 between 2 sc, ch 2, picot, ch 2, (3 dc, ch 3, 3 dc) in next corner; repeat from * 2 times more, end ch 2, picot, ch 2, (1 sc, ch 3, 1 sc) in next ch-3 between 2 sc, ch 2, picot, ch 2, join with sl st in third ch of starting ch-3.

Rnd 6: Work 1 sl st in each of next 2 dc and ch-3 sp, ch 3, (2 dc, ch 3, 3 dc) in same ch-3 sp, *ch 1, 3 dc in third dc of next 3-dc group, ch 1, 4 dc in next ch-3 sp, ch 1, 3 dc in next dc, ch 1, (3 dc, ch 3, 3 dc) in next corner

126

sp; repeat from * 2 times more, end ch 1, 3 dc in third dc of next 3-dc group, ch 1, 4 dc in next ch-3 sp, ch 1, 3 dc in next dc, ch 1, join with sl st to starting ch-3. Fasten off.

Rnd 7: With sugar plum, join in any ch-3 corner sp, ch 3, (2 dc, ch 1, picot, ch 1, 3 dc) in same ch-3 sp, *(ch 1, picot, ch 1, 3 dc in next ch-1 sp) twice, ch 1, picot, ch 1, skip 4 dc, 3 dc in next ch-1 sp, ch 1, picot, ch 1, 3 dc in next ch-1 sp, ch 1, picot, ch 1, (3 dc, ch 1, picot, ch 1, 3 dc) in next corner sp; repeat from * 2 times more, (ch 1, picot, ch 1, 3 dc in next ch-1 sp) twice, ch 1, picot, ch 1, skip 4 dc, 3 dc in next ch-1 sp, ch 1, picot, ch 1, 3 dc in next ch-1 sp, ch 1, picot, ch 1, join with sl st to third ch of starting ch-3.

To Join Additional Squares: Work as for Basic Square, and join additional squares on Rnd 7 in picots as follows: Ch 3, remove hook and insert in matching picot of adjacent square, pull dropped loop through picot, ch 1, 1 sl st in second ch of starting ch-3, ch 1, continue to work 3-dc groups between picots as established on Basic Square of Rnd 7. Join as many squares as necessary, in a strip, to go around the table. (See Note.)

Finishing: Measure crocheted strip and line with a hemmed piece of lavender fabric, leaving picot edging at top edge free. Measure a length of material 1½ times as long as crocheted strip and long enough to reach from below crocheted strip to floor. Gather long edge of material and sew to bottom edge of strip of lined crocheted squares. Cut a piece of fabric large enough to cover top of night table, allowing 1 inch for seaming all around. Sew skirt to table top.

POCKET ANIMAL NURSERY

POCKET ANIMAL BABY BLANKET

Approximate finished size: 30 by 40 inches

No experience needed

Babies love to play in their cribs for at least a few minutes after they wake up, and this crib blanket with animals should prolong the period. This unusual project features see-through pocket "cages" for a whale, a lion, and a teddy bear; the crocheted animals can also be made by themselves as hand-size gifts.

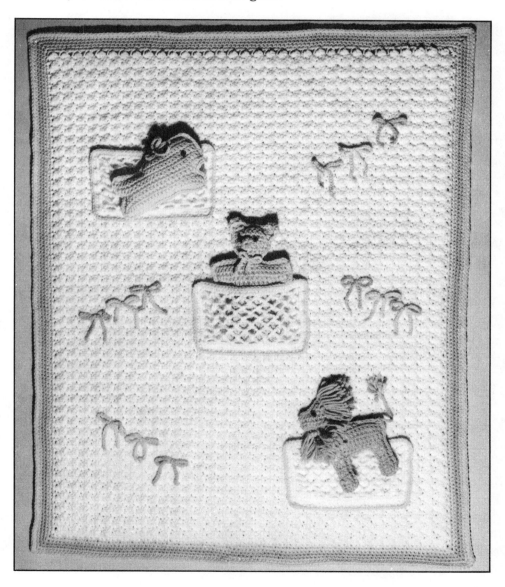

Materials:

Lion Brand Sayelle, 100-gram
  (3.5-ounce) skeins
    7 skeins color 100, white
    1 skein color 169, pastel green
    1 skein color 103, coral
    1 skein color 106, light blue

Crochet hook, size H
Polyester stuffing
Embroidery floss, in black
Embroidery needle

Gauge: 7 pattern stitches=6 inches

Pattern Stitch:
Row 1: Work 1 sc in second ch from hook, 2 dc in same ch, *skip 2 ch, (1 sc, 2 dc) in next ch—shell made; repeat from * across, ending skip 2 ch, 1 sc in last ch. Ch 1, turn.
Row 2: *Work 1 shell in next sc, skip 2 dc; repeat from * across, ending 1 sc in last sc. Ch 1, turn.
Repeat Row 2 for pat st.

Blanket: With white, ch 104. Work in pat st for 37 inches. Work 1 rnd of sc around entire piece, working 3 sc in each corner. Fasten off.

Pockets: Make 3, With white, ch 30.
Row 1: Starting in second ch from hook, work 1 sc in each ch across. Ch 1, turn.
Row 2: Work 1 sc in first sc, *ch 5, skip 3 sc, 1 sc in next sc; repeat from * across. Ch 5, turn.
Row 3: *Work 1 sc in next ch-5 loop, ch 5; repeat from * across, end 1 sc in last ch-5 loop, ch 3, 1 dc in last sc. Ch 1, turn.
Row 4: Work 1 sc in first dc, *ch 5, 1 sc in next ch-5 loop; repeat from * across, ch 5, 1 sc in third ch of turning ch-5. Ch 5, turn.
Repeat Rows 3 and 4 for 2 times more. Repeat Row 3 once more. Work Row 4 once more, but work ch 3 between sc instead of ch 5. Fasten off.

Pocket Finishing: With white, work 1 row of sc around entire piece, working 3 sc in each corner. Fasten off. With light blue, work 1 row of sc around entire piece in same manner. Fasten off. Sew to blanket, spacing

130

pockets diagonally from upper left corner to lower right corner.

Blanket Finishing: Work a border of sc around finished blanket with 2 rows of light blue, 2 rows of coral, and 2 rows of pastel green, working 3 sc in each corner on each rnd. *Bows:* Crochet four 9-inch chains in each of light blue, coral, and pastel green. Tie a bow with each chain and sew 3 bows, one of each color, diagonally in area to left of bottom pocket, right of top pocket, and both sides of center pocket.

Note: Ch 1 to turn at end of each row except where otherwise noted.

Whale: Make 2 pieces. With light blue, ch 23. Starting in second ch from hook, work in sc across. Turn. Work 1 sl st in first st, work across remaining sts in sc. Turn. *Mouth and Tail:* Work 1 sl st in each of first 3 sc, work in sc across to within last sc. Turn. Work 1 sl st in next sc, work in sc across to first of 3 sl sts, ch 5. Turn. Starting in second ch from hook, work 1 sc in each ch or sc across to within last sc, ch 4, turn. Starting in second ch from hook, work in sc for 4 rows, inc 1 st on each row at tail edge only. Sl st across first 8 sts, work in sc across. Turn. Work in sc for 3 rows more, dec 1 st at edge nearest tail on each row. Fasten off.

Whale Finishing: Work 1 row of sc around each finished piece. Place two pieces together. Crochet pieces together with sc around outside edge, leaving a small opening. Do not fasten off. Fill with stuffing. Crochet closed, join with sl st to first st. Fasten off. *Bow:* Crochet a 10-inch chain in a contrasting color and tie at top of head. *Eyes:* Embroider eyes with black yarn.

Teddy Bear: Make 2 pieces. *Leg:* With pastel green, ch 5, starting in second ch from hook, work 1 sc in each of next 4 ch. Work even on 4 sts for 8 rows. Fasten off. Make another leg in same manner. Join yarn to top corner of one leg, ch 2, join with sl st to other leg. Fasten off. Turn. Join yarn and work even in sc for 6 rows across sc sts and ch sts of both legs—10 sc. *Arms:* Ch 5, starting in second ch from hook, work 1 sc in each of next 4 ch and across next 10 sts, ch 5, turn. Starting in second ch from hook, work 1 sc in each of ch sts and 14 sc across—18 sts in all. Work even for 4 rows. *Neck:* Work 1 sl st across first 7 sts, 1 sc in each of next 4 sts. Turn. *Head:* Work in sc, inc 1 st at beg and end of every row until there are 10 sc. Work 1 row even. Now, dec 1 st at beg and end of every row until there are 4 sts. Fasten off. *Ears:* Join yarn in sc at left top of head and work 3 sc in same st. Turn. Work 1 sc in each st on next row. Turn. (Insert hook in next sc, yo, draw through) 3 times, yo, draw through all loops on hook. Fasten off. Repeat on other side of head for other ear. *Nose:* Ch 3, join with sl st to form a ring. Work 8 sc in ring, join with sl st to first st. Work 1 sc in each sc around, join with sl st to first st. Fasten off.

Teddy Bear Finishing: Sew nose in place on head. Place two finished crocheted pieces together. Crochet pieces together with sc around outside edge, leaving a small opening. Do not fasten off. Fill with stuffing. Crochet closed, join with sl st to first st. Fasten off. *Bow:* Crochet a 10-inch chain in a contrasting color and tie in bow around neck. *Eyes:* Embroider eyes with black yarn.

Lion: Make 2 pieces. *Back Leg:* With coral, ch 5. Work 1 sc in each of next 4 ch. Work 1 row even. *Paw:* Work 1 sl st in first st, work even on 3 sc for 6 rows. Fasten off. *Front Leg and Paw:* Work as for back leg and paw except work 5 rows on 3 sc instead of 6 rows. Fasten off. *Belly:* Join yarn to back leg, ch 8, join with sl st to front leg, being sure that paws are pointing in same direction. Fasten off. Working from back to front of body, join yarn and work 1 sc in each of first 3 sts, 1 sc in each of next 8 ch, 1 sc in each of next 3 sts. Turn. Work in sc for 5 rows, inc 1 st at chest edge on every other row—16 sts. *Back:* Work 1 sl st in each of next 5 sts, 1 sc in each of next 11 sts. Turn. Work 1 sl st in first st, 1 sc in each of next 5 sts, 1 sl st in next st. Turn. *Muzzle:* Work 1 sc in each of 5 sc, ch 5. Turn. Starting in second ch from hook, work 1 sc in each of next 4 ch, 1 sc in each of next 5 sc. Turn. Work 2 sc in first sc, 1 sc in each of next 8 sc. Turn. Work 1 sl st in first st, 1 sc in each of next 8 sc. Turn. Work 1 sl st in first sc, 1 sc in each of next 6 sc. Turn. Work 1 sc in each of next 5 sc. Turn. Work 1 sc in each of next 4 sc, 1 sl st in last st. Fasten off.

Lion Finishing: Place two finished crocheted pieces together. Crochet pieces together with sc around outside edge, leaving a small opening. Do not fasten off. Fill with stuffing. Crochet closed, join with sl st to first st. *Tail:* Ch 15. Fasten off. Tie four 4-inch strands, doubled, into last ch of tail. Crochet a 6-inch chain in a contrasting color and tie in a bow around the end of the tail. *Mane:* Cut 4½-inch lengths of coral yarn. Knot 3 strands, doubled, into sts around neck and head as shown in black-and-white photo. *Eyes:* Embroider eyes with black yarn.

133

POCKET ANIMAL PILLOW

Approximate finished size: 12-inch square
No experience needed

He's a baby-pink baby elephant and he fits into the "cage" in the pillow that matches the Pocket Animal Blanket that goes in the bed where baby sleeps. Make the baby elephant by itself as a soft hand toy, or get ambitious and make the pillow too.

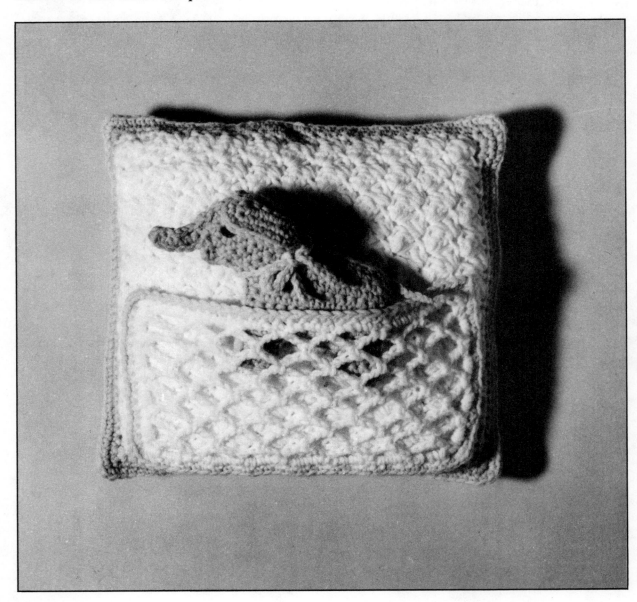

Materials:

Lion Brand Sayelle, 100-gram
(3.5-ounce) skeins
   1 skein color 100, white
   1 skein color 169, pastel green
   1 skein color 103, coral
   1 skein color 106, light blue

Crochet hook, size H
Two 14-inch pieces of fabric
Sewing thread
Polyester stuffing
Embroidery floss, in black
Embroidery needle

Gauge: 7 pattern stitches = 6 inches

Pattern Stitch:

Row 1: Work 1 sc in second ch from hook, 2 dc in same ch, *skip 2 ch, (1 sc, 2 dc) in next ch—shell made; repeat from * across, ending skip 2 ch, 1 sc in last ch. Ch 1, turn.

Row 2: *Work 1 shell in next sc, skip 2 dc; repeat from * across, ending 1 sc in last sc. Ch 1, turn.
Repeat Row 2 for pat st.

Pillow: With white, ch 35. Work in pat st for 10 inches. Work 1 rnd of sc around entire finished piece, working 3 sc in each corner. Fasten off.

Pocket: Make 1. With white, ch 30.

Row 1: Starting in second ch from hook, work 1 sc in each ch across. Ch 1, turn.

Row 2: Work 1 sc in first sc, *ch 5, skip 3 sc, 1 sc in next sc; repeat from * across. Ch 5, turn.

Row 3: *Work 1 sc in next ch-5 loop, ch 5; repeat from * across, end 1 sc in last ch-5 loop, ch 3, 1 dc in last sc. Ch 1, turn.

Row 4: Work 1 sc in first dc, *ch 5, 1 sc in next ch-5 loop; repeat from * across, ch 5, 1 sc in third ch of turning ch-5. Ch 5, turn.
Repeat Rows 3 and 4 for 2 times more. Repeat Row 3 once more. Work Row 4 once more, but work ch 3 between sc instead of ch 5. Fasten off.

Pocket Finishing: With white, work 1 row of sc around entire piece, working 3 sc in each corner. Fasten off. With light blue, work 1 row of sc in same manner. Fasten off. Center pocket on pillow and sew in place.

Pillow Finishing: Work a border of sc around finished pillow with 1 row of light blue, 1 row of coral, and 1 row of pastel green, working 3 sc in each corner on each rnd. Make a 12-inch-square pillow form from fabric, following general instructions at the beginning of the book. Sew crocheted pillow cover to pillow form.

Note: Ch 1 to turn at end of each row except where otherwise noted.

Elephant: Make 2 pieces. With coral, ch 5. *Back Leg:* Starting in second ch from hook, work 1 sc in each of next 4 ch. Turn. Work even in sc for 3 more rows. Fasten off. *Front Leg:* Work as for back leg. Do not fasten off. *Belly:* Ch 6, join with sl st to last st on last row of back leg. Fasten off. Join yarn at beg of one leg, work in sc across 4 sts of leg, 6 ch, and 4 sts of next leg. Turn. Continue in sc on all 14 sts for 8 rows more. *Back:* Work 1 sl st in each of first 2 sts at beg of row, 1 sc in each of next 2 sts, 1 hdc in each of next 5 sts, 1 sc in each of next 4 sc, 3 sc in last sc. Turn. *Neck:* Work 1 sc in each of next 6 sc. Turn. Work 1 sc in each of next 5 sc, 2 sc in next sc. Turn. Work 2 sc in first sc, 1 sc in each of next 6 sc. Turn. Work 1 sc in each of next 8 sc. *Trunk:* Ch 7, turn. Starting in second ch from hook, work 1 sc in each of next 6 ch across, 1 sc in each of next 5 sc, 1 sl st in next sc. Turn. Skip sl st, 1 sc in each of next 5 sc. Turn. Work 1 sc in each of next 5 sc, 1 sl st in next st. Turn. Work 1 sc in each of next 4 sc, 1 sl st in next st. Fasten off.

Elephant Finishing: Place two finished crocheted pieces together. Crochet together with sc around outside edge, leaving a small opening. Do not fasten off. Fill with stuffing. Crochet closed, join with sl st to first st. *Ear:* With top of elephant's head facing you, work 7 sc along top of head, inserting hook in the row one row away from joining. Work even on 7 sc for 3 rows. Fasten off. Work 1 row of sc around ear. Complete ear on other side of head in same manner. *Tail:* Join yarn to top of back end, ch 6. Fasten off. *Bow:* Crochet a 10-inch chain in a contrasting color and tie in bow around neck. *Eyes:* Embroider eyes with black yarn.

BERIBBONED DIAPER STORAGE BAG

*Approximate finished size: Bag can store up to 32 toddler-size
   disposable diapers*

No experience needed

Here's a project that's pretty and practical too. Thirty-
two toddler-size disposable diapers can be hidden away
within this diaper bag that matches the Pocket Animal
Baby Blanket and Pillow. The bag portion should be
made from a sturdy canvas-type material and stitching
should be done by machine if possible.

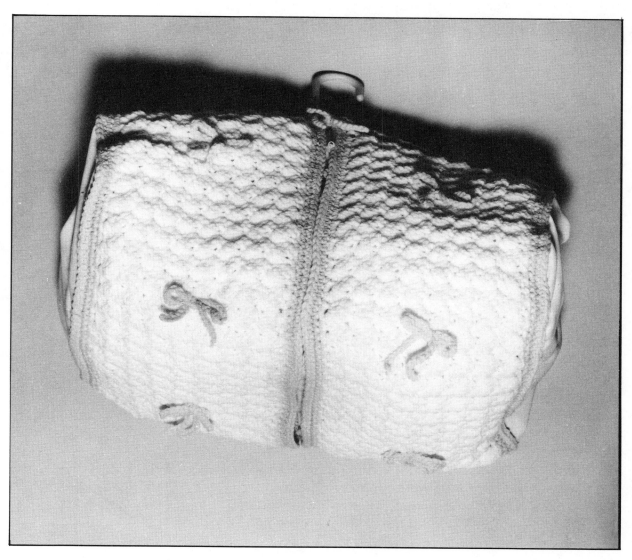

Materials:

Lion Brand Sayelle, 100-gram (3.5-ounce) skeins
- 1 skein color 100, white
- 1 skein color 169, pastel green
- 1 skein color 103, coral
- 1 skein color 106, light blue

Crochet hook, size H
Plastic hanger in matching color
1 yard cotton fabric
Sewing thread
Piece of 15- by 8-inch cardboard

Gauge: 7 pattern stitches = 6 inches

Pattern Stitch:

Row 1: Work 1 sc in second ch from hook, 2 dc in same ch, *skip 2 ch, (1 sc, 2 dc) in next ch—shell made; repeat from * across, ending skip 2 ch, 1 sc in last ch. Ch 1, turn.

Row 2: *Work 1 shell in next sc, skip 2 dc; repeat from * across, ending 1 sc in last sc. Ch 1, turn.
Repeat Row 2 for pat st.

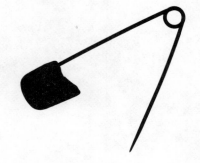

Holder Fronts: Make 2. With white, ch 26. Work in pat st for 20 inches. Work 1 rnd of sc around entire finished piece, working 3 sc in each corner. Fasten off.

Finishing: *Edging:* Work a border of sc around the finished pieces with 1 row of light blue, 1 row of coral, and 1 row of pastel green, working 3 sc in each corner on each rnd. Cut back and two side pieces of fabric as shown in the diagram, adding 1/2 inch all around. Use your own hanger as a pattern for the top triangular section of the back/bottom piece, allowing extra material to fold over the sloping sides of hanger. With right sides together and allowing 1/2 inch for the seam, sew the side fabric pieces to the back/bottom fabric piece. Place the hanger on the top section of bag, fold the fabric over the sloping sides of the hanger toward the inside of the bag, and sew in place. Sew the crocheted pieces in place to the bottom edge, sides, and top edge of the fabric bag. *Bows:* Crochet two 9-inch chains in each of light blue, coral, and pastel green. Tie a bow with each chain and sew the three bows in place, spaced evenly on each crocheted piece, alternating colors. Make two more 6-inch chains in pastel green and attach one to the top inside corner of each crocheted piece; tie in a bow.

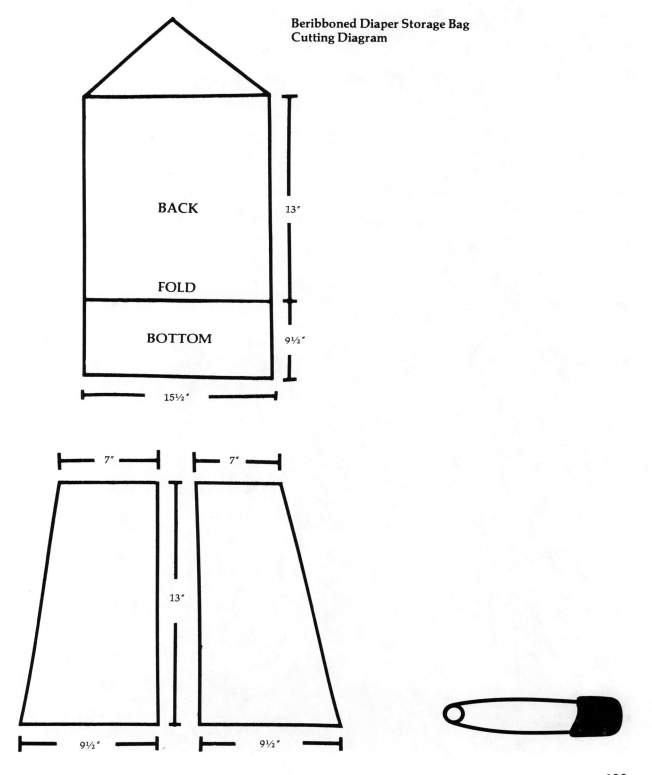

Beribboned Diaper Storage Bag
Cutting Diagram

BACK

13″

FOLD

BOTTOM

9½″

15½″

7″

7″

13″

9½″

9½″

139

CROCHETED PROJECTS
FOR ON-THE-GO

BARGELLO LAP ROBE

Approximate finished size: 40 by 50 inches
Some experience needed

The bargello-like stitch that decorates this project is achiev-
ed by working single-crochet stitches, in graduating
steps, into stitches in the rows below. Be sure not
to gather up the rows below by working over
them too tightly. The lap robe can be folded up into a
compact roll and tied with its own double-crochet "belt."

Materials:
Aunt Lydia's Heavy Rug Yarn, 60-yard (1.37-ounce) skeins
    17 skeins color 405, beige
     9 skeins color 635, light avocado
     6 skeins color 310, coral
Crochet hook, size K

Gauge: 11 single crochet = 4 inches

Strips: Make 3. With beige, ch 34.
Row 1: Starting in second ch from hook, work 1 sc in each st across—33 sc.
Rows 2 through 8: Work in sc on 33 sts.
Row 9: With light avocado, work 1 sc in first st, work in sc across, inserting hook for each sc, respectively, *1 row below next sc, 2 rows below next sc, 3 rows below next sc, 4 rows below next sc, 3 rows below next sc, 2 rows below next sc; repeat from * 4 times more, insert hook for next sc 1 row below next sc, end 1 sc in last st.
Row 10: Work 1 row with light avocado in sc.
Rows 11 and 12: Work 2 rows sc with coral.
Rows 13 through 20: Work 8 rows sc with beige.
Repeat Rows 9 through 20 for 11 times more, end with Rows 9 through 16. Fasten off.

Finishing: With light avocado and single crochet, join strips. With light avocado, work 1 row of sc around entire joined piece, working 3 sc in each corner.

Tie: With light avocado, ch 92. Starting in third ch from hook, work 1 dc in each ch across. Fasten off. Fold side panels in toward center, roll folded piece, and wrap with tie.

BARGELLO SHAWL

Approximate finished size: 16 by 60 inches
Some experience needed

The same stitch that decorates the Bargello Lap Robe is used here in a different combination of colors. A bulky yarn was chosen because we expect this shawl to have outdoor use, but the same pattern could be made with lighter-weight yarns.

Materials:
Aunt Lydia's Heavy Rug Yarn, 60-yard (1.37-ounce) skeins
 11 skeins color 635, light avocado
 3 skeins color 310, coral
Crochet hook, size K

Gauge: 5 single crochet = 2 inches

Shawl: With light avocado, ch 41.
Row 1: Starting in second ch from hook, work 1 sc in each st across—40 sc.
Rows 2 through 8: Work in sc on 40 sts.
Row 9: With coral, work 1 sc in first st, work in sc across, inserting hook for each sc st, respectively, *1 row below next sc, 2 rows below next sc, 3 rows below next sc, 4 rows below next sc, 3 rows below next sc, 2 rows below next sc; repeat from * 5 times more, end working each sc st 1 row below next sc, 2 rows below next sc, 1 sc in last sc. Ch 1, turn.
Row 10: Work with coral in sc.
Rows 11 through 18: Work in sc with light avocado.
Repeat Rows 9 through 18 for 18 times more, end with Rows 9 through 14. Fasten off.

Finishing: With light avocado, work 2 rows of sc along each long edge.

Fringe: Cut 8-inch strands of light avocado. Knot 4 strands in every other st across both short edges of shawl.

BARGELLO TRAVEL PILLOW

Approximate finished size: 17 by 14 inches
Some experience needed

This pillow coordinates with the Bargello Lap Robe and
Shawl in our crocheted set that makes winter traveling a
pleasure. The pillow can be enhanced with the addition
of a fabric pocket sewn onto the back of the pillow to
hold a paperback book, a deck of playing cards, or a
road map.

Materials:
Aunt Lydia's Heavy Rug Yarn, 60-yard (1.37-ounce) skeins
    3 skeins color 310, coral
    1 skein color 635, light avocado
Crochet hook, size K
Two 15- by 18-inch pieces of fabric, in coordinating
    color
Polyester stuffing
Sewing thread

Gauge: 5 single crochet = 2 inches

Shawl: With coral, ch 44.
Row 1: Starting in second ch from hook, work 1 sc in each st across—43 sc.
Rows 2 through 8: Work in sc on 43 sts.
Row 9: With light avocado, work 1 sc in first st, work in sc across, inserting hook for each sc st, respectively, *1 row below next sc, 2 rows below next sc, 3 rows below next sc, 4 rows below next sc, 3 rows below next sc, 2 rows below next sc; repeat from * 5 times more, end working each sc st 1 row below next sc, 2 rows below next sc, 3 rows below next sc, 4 rows below next sc, 3 rows below next sc, 1 sc in last st.
Row 10: Work with light avocado in sc.
Rows 11 through 18: Work in sc with coral.
Repeat Rows 9 through 18 for 2 times more, end with Rows 9 through 14. Fasten off.

Finishing: With coral, work 1 row of sc around entire piece, working 3 sc in each corner. Make a pillow form 17 inches by 14 inches, following general instructions in the beginning of the book. Sew crocheted pillow cover to pillow form.

STITCH GLOSSARY

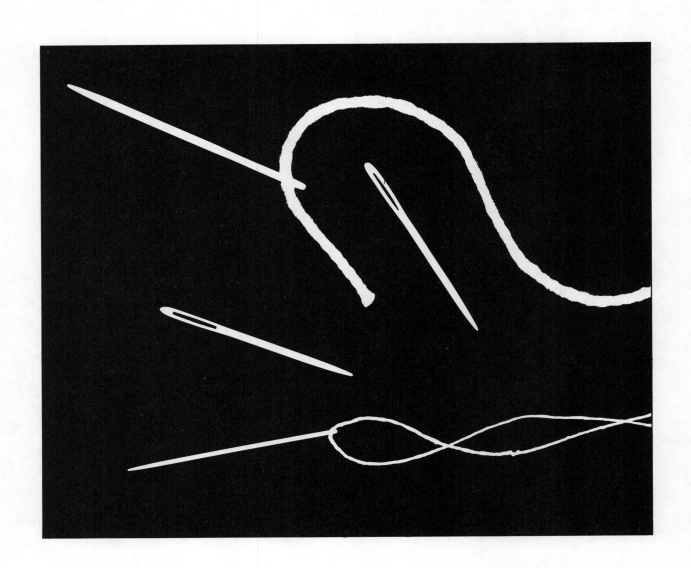

CROCHETING

Foundation Chain (ch)

Knot a slip loop onto the hook (A). Hold the hook in your right hand and place the long end of the yarn to be used over the index finger of the left hand, under the next two fingers, and loosely around the little finger. *Place the end of the hook under the length of yarn (this is called yarn over—yo), catch the yarn with the hook (B), and pull the yarn through the loop onto the shaft of the hook. Repeat this process from the * as many times as specified in the directions.

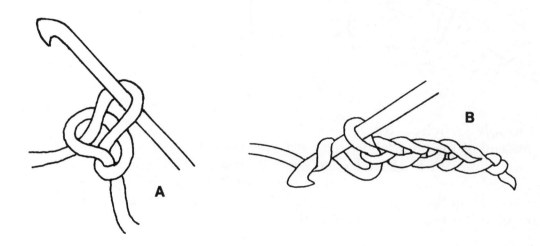

Slip Stitch (sl st)

Insert the hook under the two top strands of the stitch to be worked, place the end of the hook under the yarn (this is called yarn over—yo), catch the yarn with the hook, and pull the yarn through the stitch and the loop on the hook in one motion.

Single Crochet (sc)

Insert the hook under the two top strands of the stitch to be worked, place the end of the hook under the yarn (this is called yarn over—yo), catch the yarn with the hook and pull the yarn through the stitch (two loops are now on the hook); yarn over and pull the yarn through the two loops on the hook.

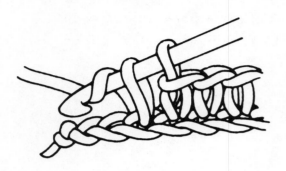

Half Double Crochet (hdc)

Place the end of the hook under the yarn (this is called yarn over—yo), insert the hook under the two top strands of the stitch to be worked; yarn over and pull the yarn through the stitch (three loops are now on the hook); yarn over and pull the yarn through all three loops on the hook in one motion.

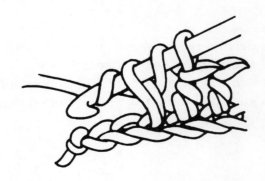

Double Crochet (dc)

Place the end of the hook under the yarn (this is called yarn over—yo), insert the hook under the two top strands of the stitch to be worked; yarn over and pull the yarn through the stitch (three loops are now on the hook); yarn over and pull the yarn through the first two loops on the hook; yarn over once more and pull the yarn through the remaining two loops on the hook.

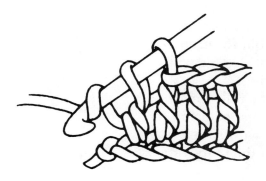

Treble Crochet (tr)

Place the end of the hook under the yarn (this is called yarn over—yo), yarn over once more and insert the hook under the two top strands of the stitch to be worked; yarn over and pull the yarn through the stitch (there are now four loops on the hook); yarn over and pull the yarn through the first two loops on the hook (three loops are now on the hook); yarn over again and pull the yarn through the next two loops on the hook (two loops are now on the hook); yarn over once more and pull the yarn through the last two loops on the hook.

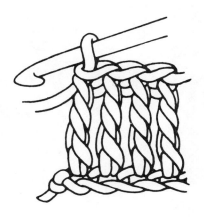

To Increase or Decrease (inc or dec)

In this book, the type of decrease or increase to be used, if any, is specified in the directions.

Changing Color in Crochet

For a pattern that incorporates two or more colors throughout, there are two ways to change from one color to another: (1) If the colors are used interchangeably throughout, loosely carry along the unused yarns behind the work or work over the unused colors while they lie across the top of the previous row; (2) If colors are worked only in specified areas, wind a separate bobbin for each of those colors and use the ball of yarn for the main color. This will eliminate the need for carrying colors along the work.

In either case, while working across a piece, use the following method to change color. Work the last stitch of the first color up to the last yarn over drawn through, hold the first color to the left, yarn over with the second color, and pull it through the loops on the hook to finish the stitch. Continue working with the second color, carrying the unused yarn as previously explained.

KNITTING

To Cast On

Make a slip loop on your needle (A) about 2 yards (per 100 stitches to be cast on) from the end of the yarn. Hold the needle in your right hand with the 2-yard end of the yarn closest to you, *make a loop around your left-hand thumb with 2-yard end and insert the needle from front to back through this loop (B). Wrap the yarn, extending from the skein or ball, under and around the needle (C). Pull the yarn, using the end of the needle, through the loop, and pull the 2-yard end down to tighten it around the needle (D). Repeat from * for the specified number of stitches.

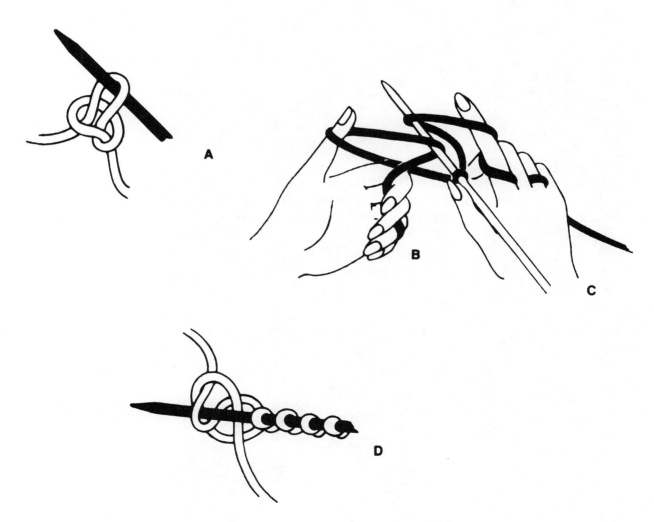

To Knit (k)

Hold the needle with the cast-on stitches in your left hand with the yarn in back of the work, *insert the right needle from left to right through the front of the first stitch, wrap the yarn under and around the right needle to form a loop, pull the tip of the right needle and the loop just made on it through the stitch on the left needle toward the front, and then slip the original stitch off the left needle; repeat from * across the stitches on the left needle.

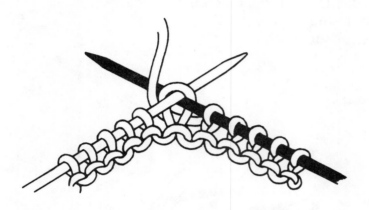

To Purl (p)

Hold the needle with the cast-on stitches in your left hand with the yarn in front of the work, *insert the right needle from right to left through the front of the first stitch on the left needle. Wrap the yarn around the right needle to form a loop, pull the tip of the right needle and the loop just made through the stitch toward the back, and then slip the original stitch off the left needle; repeat from * across the stitches on the left needle.

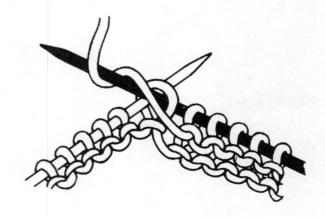

To Bind Off

Knit or purl, as specified, the first 2 stitches. Then *insert the point of the left needle into the first stitch on the right needle (A) and lift this stitch over the second stitch and off the right needle completely (B). Knit or purl the next stitch. Repeat from * for the number of stitches specified. When all the stitches are to be bound off and you reach the point at which there is only 1 stitch left, cut the yarn and draw the end of the yarn through the stitch.

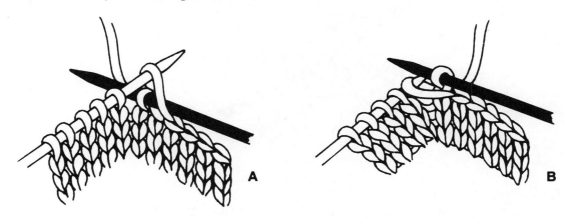

To Increase (inc)

When knitting, knit the stitch in which the increase is to be worked in the usual manner, but do not remove from the left needle; work a knit stitch in the back loop of the same stitch and slip the original stitch off the left needle. When purling, purl the stitch in which the increase is to be worked in the usual manner, but do not remove from the left needle; bring the yarn to the back of the work, work a knit stitch in the back loop of the same stitch, and slip the original stitch off the left needle.

To Decrease (dec) or (k 2 or p 2 tog)

Insert the right needle, either to purl or to knit, as specified, through 2 stitches and work through these 2 stitches together as one.

Slip Stitch (sl st) or (sl 1 as if to p)

Insert the right needle from right to left through the front of the stitch to be slipped and transfer it to the right needle without working it.

Pass Slip Stitch Over (psso)

Lift the slipped stitch on the right needle with the point of the left needle, pass it over the specified number of stitches and the tip of the right needle, and drop it.

Yarn Over (yo)

To work a yarn over, wrap the yarn around the tip of the right needle once, or as many times as specified, to create an additional loop, or loops, on the right needle, which will be either knitted into on the next row to increase by 1 stitch or dropped to create an elongated stitch.

Changing Color in Knitting

If you are working stripes, carry the unused yarn along one edge of the work by twisting it around the yarn in use at the end of each row at that edge.

If many colors are being used but they are confined to one area, use bobbins for each color except the main one. When changing colors, twist the two yarns once and then work across, using the second color while carrying the main color loosely across the back of the work by twisting it with the working color every 5 to 8 stitches.

If only two or three colors are being used alternately throughout, carry the unworked colors loosely across the back, twisting them one at a time with the main color every 5 to 8 stitches and twisting at the stitch just before the color change is made.

EMBROIDERY AND SEWING

Duplicate Stitch

Following the chart provided with the instructions for the design, bring the yarn up, from wrong to right side, through the center of the base of a knit stitch. Insert the needle into the top of the right side of the same stitch and pass it through horizontally to the top of the left side of the same stitch. Insert the needle again into the center of the base of the stitch. Pull the yarn through with a light tension so that the yarn completely covers the stitch being embroidered.

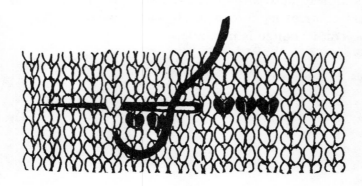

Running Back Stitch

Work from right to left. Hold the pieces together with right sides facing and work through both thicknesses. Bring thread up through point A, insert it at point B, and bring it out again at point C. Continue to work in this manner.

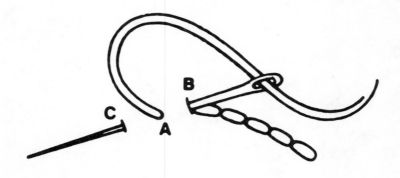

Overcast Stitch

Hold the two pieces edge to edge, matching them stitch for stitch, and bring the thread or yarn through both pieces in one motion, as shown.

The text of this book is set in paladium

Composition by Valley Graphics
Printed and bound by R.R. Donnelley and Sons Company
Color printing by Eastern Press
Color separation by South China Printing Company